The Mentor's Handbook:

Practical Suggestions for Collaborative Reflection and Analysis

The Mentor's Handbook:

Practical Suggestions for Collaborative Reflection and Analysis

Marlene P. Correia

Jana M. McHenry

Christopher-Gordon Publishers, Inc.
Norwood, Massachusetts

Copyright Acknowledgments

The Bill Harp Professional Teacher's Library
An Imprint of
Christopher-Gordon Publishers, Inc.
1502 Providence Highway, Suite 12
Norwood, MA 02062
800-934-8322

Printed in the United States of America

10 9 8 7 6 5 4 3 2 1   05 04 03 02 01

Library of Congress Catalog Card Number: 2001098945
ISBN: 1-929024-44-4

To beginning teachers,
and those who choose to mentor them.

Contents

Preface

The Mentor's Handbook: Practical Suggestions for Collaborative Reflection and Analysis is meant to serve, as the name implies, as a handbook. It offers practical strategies for mentors to implement easily and effectively when in a mentoring relationship, yet it is flexible enough to tailor to your own personal situation.

Chapter 1, "Wanted: Mentor," defines the word *mentor* and explores the need for mentoring.

Chapter 2, "The Cycle of Conferencing," outlines a discussion process that includes the components of collaborative reflection and analysis, preconferencing, observation and data gathering, and postconferencing. In addition, the chapter offers guiding questions for a preconference and postconference as well as a vignette illustrating the conferences in action.

Chapters 3 through 7 focus on five observation techniques: Word for Word, Keeping Track of Time, Mapping the Classroom: Movement and Materials, Measuring Methodology, and the Sights and Sounds of the Classroom. You may already be familiar with the value of some of these techniques (e.g., videotaping), but these chapters present how they can be effective tools for the mentor to use in observing and providing feedback to a mentee. Each chapter provides an overview of the technique, examples of how the technique can be used, and a vignette illustrating the technique in action. Each chapter concludes with questions to encourage collaborative reflection between mentor and mentee.

Chapter 8, "The Link to Standards," provides suggestions for how mentors can aid their new teachers in collecting evidence that they have met the required standards through the observations techniques outlined in this book and other methods that are appropriate to individual situations. The link to collecting and documenting this evidence in a professional portfolio is also discussed. Finally, a list of Web sites of professional organizations, with standards links, is included for further investigation based on personal needs and interests.

Chapter 9, "The Link to Professional Development," offers suggestions for the type of professional development a mentor and mentee can engage in together. This chapter also reaffirms the benefit that professional development can provide for both teachers.

Chapter 10, "A Mentor and Mentee in Action," provides an inside look into the world of mentoring. Through a personal interview, a mentor-mentee team shares its thoughts on the mentoring program as well as the highlights and challenges of the mentoring relationship.

Finally, Chapter 11, "Putting It All Together," summarizes the importance of mentoring and the role of the mentor. Some concluding advice for mentors as well as resources for further investigation are also provided.

We believe that mentors are not evaluators but coaches who provide guidance and capitalize on the mentee's strengths in the classroom. As you guide your mentee through those first few difficult years of teaching, we hope this handbook will prove to be a beneficial resource for both of you.

Acknowledgments

We are thankful to have Christopher-Gordon Publishers recognize the timeliness and need for a handbook for mentors. In addition, we are privileged to have studied under the guidance of Dr. William Harp at the University of Massachusetts Lowell, who supported our ideas and encouraged us through the process.

We are also appreciative of the time, experiences, and advice shared by special educators Leonore Rizy and Erica Bulk in our interview with them for Chapter 10.

We would like to acknowledge the people in our professional lives who have mentored us in some way. They include our colleagues at Salve Regina University, the faculty at the University of Massachusetts Lowell Graduate School of Education, and other educators and students who have enriched our professional experiences.

Heartfelt thanks also extend to our mutual friend, Julie Andrade, for her encouragement and suggestions.

Most important, we could not have written this book amid all the other responsibilities in our lives without the support of our wonderful families. We would like to recognize the countless times our husbands, Brian and Michael, have unselfishly given of themselves to clean, cook, care for the children, and provide lots of love and care for the two of us. We are also very fortunate to have young children (Alyssa, Jillian, and Caitlin) who inspire us to set high expectations for those who teach children. We acknowledge our daughters for the time they spent entertaining themselves patiently while Mom was writing.

Wanted: Mentor

Figure 1-1. Want Ad for Mentor

WANTED

Mentor Wanted for New Teacher

Qualifications:

- Dedication to the field of education
- Professionally developed
- Knowledge of standards
- Willingness to help others
- Objective
- Reflective
- Patient

Responsibilities:

- Establishing a relationship with a mentee
- Engaging in collaborative reflection and analysis
- Conducting observations
- Sharing time and resources
- Fostering professional development
- Offering emotional support
- Encouraging self-reliance

Persons interested in this position should consult the following:
The Mentor's Handbook:
Practical Suggestions for Collaborative Reflection and Analysis

Are you interested in the position described in Figure 1-1? Chances are that if you are reading this book, you are interested in becoming a mentor, or perhaps you are already a mentor and would like to strengthen your role in this capacity. This book is designed to support you as you embark on or continue in a mentoring relationship.

As you think back to your first teaching experience, can you recall some of the emotions you felt? Nervous, excited, anxious, alone? Those of you who have been teaching for a while may have encountered a caring colleague who would offer practical advice and moral support. However, you probably did not encounter a "mentor": someone who would confer, observe, and collaboratively analyze and reflect; who would assist you in setting and meeting personal goals as well as fulfilling local and national standards; and who would foster your professional development.

What Is a Mentor?

In the field of education, the term *mentor* is associated with many ideas. Mentors are sometimes referred to as coaches, guides, models, teachers, and trainers. Holden (1995) offers the following definitions of a mentor:

- A mentor is a teacher of teachers.
- A mentor is an experienced, successful, and knowledgeable professional who willingly accepts the responsibility of facilitating professional growth and support of a colleague through a mutually beneficial relationship.
- A mentor is a friend with a positive attitude and a sense of humor.
- A mentor is an experienced teacher whose willingness to assist and support new teachers is readily apparent in his or her attitudes, beliefs, and philosophies about teaching.
- A mentor is sensitive, discreet, wise, knowledgeable, and caring. (p. 2)

Lyons & Pinnell (2001) refer to the role of the "more expert other," who:

- Gives us an idea of what success looks like—just beyond our present expertise.
- Suggests next steps to take in our learning.
- Helps to break down complex processes so that we can see and practice parts if necessary.
- Helps us to keep the big picture in mind so that we can orchestrate components of a process.
- Offers support and encouragement.
- Identifies critical junctures and provides help at those times.
- Helps us evaluate the outcome and realize improvement.
- Restarts the process at a higher level. (p. 140)

Regardless of these various terms, definitions, and roles associated with a mentor, the need for mentors remains a constant.

The Need for Mentors

Why are mentors so important? Teaching, by nature, is different from any other profession.

> [B]eginners in teaching are expected to do essentially the same job on the first day of employment as the 20-year veteran. In addition, teachers spend the majority of their workday isolated from their peers....Furthermore, beginning teachers are often given some of the most difficult teaching assignments. (Holden, 1995, p. 1)

With circumstances such as these, it is no wonder so many new teachers abandon the profession. In fact, now more than ever, there is a strong rationale for mentoring.

> A baby boomlet combined with a retirement boom will result in a need for 2 million new teachers in the next 10 years. The cost of preparing and recruiting teachers grows higher in light of the statistic that tells us that 30 percent of newcomers will quit within their first five years in the classroom. (Scherer, 1999, p. 7)

This delicate balance of supply and demand leaves the field of education vulnerable. In response, many states are mandating beginning teacher support systems, such as mentoring. This, in turn, creates an additional need: to support mentors as they strive to support these new teachers.

Final Thoughts

The following chapters are meant to aid in this process of mutual support. Practical suggestions for mentor and mentee to engage in conferences, observations, addressing standards, and professional development are presented, with collaborative reflection and analysis as the foundation.

We applaud your commitment to the field of education by answering this want ad to support these new teachers, thus improving education for all students.

References

Holden, J. (1995). *Mentoring frameworks for Texas teachers.* (ERIC Document Reproduction Service No. ED 398 227)

Lyons, C. A., & Pinnell, G. S. (2001). *Systems for change in literacy education: A guide to professional development.* Portsmouth, NH: Heinemann.

Scherer, M. (1999). Perspectives: Knowing how and knowing why. *Educational Leadership, 56* (8), 7.

2

The Cycle of Conferencing

"New teachers who engage in the developmental cycle of planning, teaching, reflecting, and applying what they have learned are on the road to becoming competent practitioners" (Lucas, 1999, p. 47). One way a mentor can assist a new teacher to engage in these activities is through conferencing. Conferencing

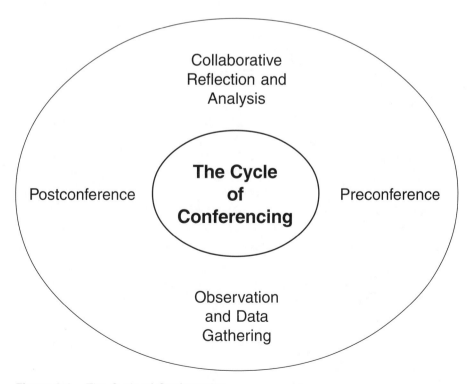

Figure 2-1. The Cycle of Conferencing

is an essential component in the mentoring relationship. A typical conferencing format includes a preconference, an observation, and a postconference. Mentor and mentee initially meet to discuss the parameters for an observation; the mentor conducts a classroom observation; then they meet to discuss the results. In our Cycle of Conferencing (Fig. 2-1), however, we suggest another phase: collaborative reflection and analysis. This phase actually permeates each of the other phases. It is the momentum that feeds the cycle, it concludes one cycle as well as begins the next, and it could even be considered the binding that holds this book together.

Collaborative Reflection and Analysis

Collaborative reflection and analysis is an ongoing process. "The ordinary experiences of our teaching days are the essence of our practice" (Hole & McEntee, 1999, p. 34). For novice and seasoned teachers alike, each day of teaching provides food for thought. This reflection is cumulative in nature; we learn from each new experience and can apply our knowledge to our practice as well as our future deliberations.

Reflection, however, is not something that just happens; it is an active process. "If one holds a constructivist view of learning, in which the learner actively constructs meaning according to what he or she already knows and believes, it follows that good teaching must itself involve learning through active enquiry" (Baird, 1992, p. 36). For true reflection and analysis, we must actively move beyond the surface: What is the issue? We must look deeper: Why is this an issue? What are my own beliefs and attitudes regarding this issue? What are other possible sides to the issue? What are possible action plans for resolving this issue? How can I evaluate the effectiveness of my action plan? What have I learned from this process? Additionally, engaging in *collaborative* reflection requires not only looking beyond the surface but also looking beyond ourselves.

Collaborative reflection and analysis can take many forms. Mentor and mentee can engage in a conversation, spontaneously or at a planned meeting; examine oral or written feedback from an administrator or students; analyze notes from an observed lesson; write in a personal or dialogue journal; or research a particular area of interest. Regardless of the type(s) of reflection you and your mentee engage in, collaborative reflection and analysis that is ongoing and active will foster thoughtful, purposeful practitioners. Ultimately, it will be the students who reap the most benefit from this process.

The Preconference

The next phase in the Cycle of Conferencing is the preconference. Table 2-1 lists pre-conference guiding questions. These are provided as samples and can easily be revised to suit your individual situation and style.

Table 2-1. Preconference Guiding Questions

- What are your objectives for the lesson?

- In what particular area would you like me to observe and collect data (e.g., giving directions, wait time for student responses, monitoring group work)?

- Will this lesson provide evidence that you are meeting required standards? If so, which standards relate to this particular lesson?

- How will you assess the students' growth as related to your lesson objectives?

- How will you evaluate your role in this lesson?

- _____

- _____

- _____

Generally, the preconference should address the objectives or purpose of the lesson, the area(s) which the new teacher identifies as a concern, the link to standards (see chapter 8), the student assessment procedures, and the role of teacher self-reflection and evaluation. Once you have discussed these areas, the scheduled observation can be conducted.

Observation and Data Gathering

The second phase in the Cycle of Conferencing is observation and data gathering. Following the preconference session, the mentor conducts an observation of the mentee in order to gather data to be discussed in the postconference session. It is important to remember that the mentor's role is to focus on the area that the mentee identified as a concern in the preconference session. Does that mean you can't discuss a different issue that caught your attention during the observation? Of course not. You are a professional and need to use your professional discretion for matters such as these. Just be sure you are wearing a "mentor's hat" and not an "evaluator's hat"; that is, offer the comment in the spirit of collaborative reflection.

Depending on the area of concern identified by your mentee, you can choose from one of the observation techniques presented in this book or perhaps design one of your own. Table 2-2 lists the observation techniques described in this book and provides space for you to personalize the list by adding techniques of your own.

Table 2-2. Observation Techniques for Data Gathering

- Word for Word

- Keeping Track of Time

- Mapping the Classroom: Movement and Materials

- Measuring Methodology

- The Sights and Sounds of the Classroom

- _____

- _____

Word for Word is useful when your mentee identifies his or her oral communication skills as an area of concern. With this technique, the mentor writes down exactly what the new teacher says, word for word, within a particular category (see chapter 3).

Keeping Track of Time can assist in the observation of a mentee's time management skills. The mentor records how much time the teacher spends on a specific part or various parts of the instruction (see chapter 4).

Mapping the Classroom: Movement and Materials can provide information on the presence and use of movement and materials in the classroom. Through "formal" diagrams and informally surveying the classroom, the mentor and mentee can analyze aspects of the physical environment, including teacher and student movement (see chapter 5).

Measuring Methodology is appropriate for examining the variety of methods employed by the mentee. As an observation checklist or a self-assessment tool, this technique offers insight into the teacher's methodology (see chapter 6).

The Sights and Sounds of the Classroom utilizes video- and audiotaping as observation tools. With these tools, the mentor and mentee can reflect upon and analyze a host of issues regarding teacher as well as student behavior (see chapter 7).

Through observation techniques such as these, both mentor and mentee can collaboratively and objectively reflect upon and analyze the data gathered during the lesson. This data provides the basis for discussion during the postconference session.

The Postconference

The next phase in the Cycle of Conferencing is the postconference. Table 2-3 lists postconference guiding questions. Similar to the preconference questions, these are examples that can be adjusted to meet the needs of you and your mentee.

Table 2-3. Postconference Guiding Questions

- What were the strengths of your lesson? What areas may need improvement?
- Were the objectives of the lesson met?
- Let's review the data I collected. What do you notice?
- Do you have evidence from your lesson that you met the required standards that you identified in our preconference session? How will you document this evidence?
- Is there a goal you would like to set for future lessons? What is a possible action plan for achieving this goal?
- When should we meet again to reevaluate this goal or investigate another area?
- _____
- _____
- _____

These questions should complement the preconference questions. In addition, they are meant to extend beyond the observation by setting a goal, devising an action plan to meet that goal, and considering a follow-up to assess progress. Notice, however, that the questions are designed to foster a *conversation* between two people rather than an individual's report of his or her observations accompanied by a list of "expert" advice.

Lyons & Pinnell (2001) offer five essential features for an effective coaching conversation. Although their focus is on a literacy staff developer and a teacher, these features are most appropriate for this phase of the Cycle of Conferencing as well.

1. It is tied to a specific event that has just occurred.
2. It takes place in the context of the teacher's attempt to learn a specific technique or concept.
3. It makes use of specific teacher and student actions as well as words.
4. It includes reciprocal reflection and constructive dialogue between teacher and coach.

5. It results in new learning and a plan of action to improve teaching. (p. 141)

These five features easily translate to the conferencing situation. The observed lesson serves as the "specific event." The "technique or concept" to be learned is synonymous with the area of concern identified by the mentee. The observation technique employed by the mentor focuses on teacher and student "actions" and "words." The postconference guiding questions encourage "reciprocal reflection and constructive dialogue." Finally, the setting of a goal for the mentee is followed by "a plan of action to improve teaching." These features offer sound advice for maintaining collaboration during this aspect of the mentoring relationship.

A Preconference in Action

It is Jill's second year of teaching. She has spent both last year and this year teaching the fifth grade at an elementary school quite some distance from her home. As she commutes to school each morning, she often informally reflects on her teaching. Now, with a year of experience, she feels so much more comfortable with certain aspects of the job, such as establishing schedules and routines, planning for her classes, and even implementing some effective classroom management techniques. She had learned a lot her first year, and she was particularly grateful for the help of her mentor. There are, however, certain aspects of the job that still concern her. Lately, she has been questioning how effectively she is managing the class when they work in small groups. Is she attending to each group's needs? Does she consistently visit the groups to keep them on task or extend their thinking? Jill decided these would be appropriate questions for the next preconference session with her mentor.

Jill and her mentor met and followed the Preconference Guiding Questions (see Table 2-1) to structure their session. Jill shared her objectives for a social studies lesson on the Declaration of Independence. The students had been studying the American Revolution. By having her students revisit a chapter in their textbook, she wanted them to work in small groups to create a time line of events leading up to the signing of the Declaration of Independence.

She discussed with her mentor her concerns about managing small-group work and asked her mentor to collect data specifically in this area. They decided together that a combination of two observation techniques, Mapping the Classroom: Movement and Materials (see chapter 5) and Keeping Track of Time (see chapter 4), would be most appropriate for providing feedback in this area. During the observation, the mentor would mark a tally beside each group whenever Jill visited it and would also record how much time she spent with each group.

After examining the INTASC Core Standards together (see chapter 8), Jill identified Principle No. 5 ("The teacher uses an understanding of individual and group motivation and behavior to create a learning environment that encourages positive social interaction, active engagement in learning, and self-motivation") as being met by this lesson.

Jill planned to collect the time lines and have students summarize the information from their time line in their content journal at the end of the lesson. She would then collect the journals and read the responses to assess the students' growth and plan her future lessons on this topic. As the students wrote in their journals, she would write in her own reflective journal to evaluate her role in the lesson and note possible questions and comments for her postconference session with her mentor.

The observation was to take place at the end of the week, and after school that same day Jill and her mentor would meet to discuss the results.

A Postconference in Action

Jill and her mentor met after the observation, as planned, and followed the Postconference Guiding Questions (see Table 2-3) to structure their session. From time to time, Jill would consult her reflective journal.

Jill's mentor asked her to discuss the strengths and the areas that may need improvement in the lesson. Jill stated she was actually quite pleased with the lesson. She believed that the lesson was well planned, that her instructions were clear, and that she had indeed attended to each of the small groups. On the other hand, she was still concerned with the students' on-task and off-task behavior as she attended to other groups. They seemed to be on task, but how could she be sure?

Jill and her mentor also discussed how well the students had met the lesson objectives. Although Jill had not yet had the time to thoroughly read the time lines or journal responses, she had skimmed through them. From the student discussions she had observed and from her preliminary reactions to the time lines and journals, she believed that the objectives were met. However, she would need more time to completely assess the journal entries.

Jill and her mentor then reviewed the data that was collected during the lesson:

Group	# of Visits	Total Time
1	2	6 minutes
2	2	6½ minutes
3	3	7 minutes
4	2	5 minutes
5	2	6½ minutes

The data showed that she had visited each group a total of 2 to 3 times and had spent between 5 to 7 minutes with each group. Jill was relieved to see that she was distributing her attention among all the groups.

Because Jill had accomplished some successful group work in the lesson, she decided to use her lesson plan along with her mentor's notes from the observation as evidence of having met INTASC Core Standards Principle No. 5, as she had identified in the preconference session. She would include these evidences in her portfolio. For additional feedback and documentation, Jill's mentor suggested having the students provide a written response on the small-group process. Jill liked this idea very much and planned to try this approach in a future lesson.

It was now time for Jill to set a goal. Although she was pleased with her management of the small groups, she still questioned the students' on-task and off-task behavior during this time. Therefore, she devised an action plan to incorporate a few minutes of observing all the students interacting in the small groups rather than spending each free minute within a group. Her mentor thought this was a sound plan and suggested that they reevaluate this area in about a month. They both decided that the mentor could videotape the next lesson (see chapter 7), which would provide data on Jill's management of the groups as well as her students' on-task and off-task behavior. Jill's mentor also brought a copy of an article she had recently read on effective management of cooperative learning groups (see chapter 9), which could offer some additional information and suggestions.

Jill smiled at the end of the session, for she felt reaffirmed in her competence as a teacher; Jill's mentor smiled at the end of the session, too, for she felt reaffirmed in her competence as a mentor.

References

Baird, J. R. (1992). Collaborative reflection, systematic enquiry, better teaching. In T. Russell & H. Munby (Eds.), *Teachers and teaching: From classroom to reflection* (pp. 33–48). New York: Falmer Press.

Hole, S., & McEntee, G. H. (1999). Reflection is at the heart of practice. *Educational Leadership,* 56 (8), 34–40.

Lucas, C. A. (1999). Developing competent practitioners. *Educational Leadership, 56* (8), 45–48.

Lyons, C. A., & Pinnell, G. S. (2001). *Systems for change in literacy education: A guide to professional development.* Portsmouth, NH: Heinemann.

Chapter

3

Observation Technique
No. 1: Word for Word

The ability to communicate effectively is essential to teaching. Communication skills, however, may provide some of the most difficult challenges for the new teacher. Let's suppose that your mentee identified his or her ability to give clear directions as a particular area of concern. How do you, as the mentor, provide appropriate feedback? You don't want the new teacher to feel as though your suggestions are only your opinion or are blinded in any way by your own teaching style and beliefs. On the other hand, you don't want your compliments to be "empty" and seem trivial. By using Word for Word, you can collect factual evidence right from the lesson you observe. Then, along with the mentee, you can collaboratively analyze and reflect upon the results.

What Is Word for Word?

Word for Word is an observation technique that is useful in observing and collecting data based on the mentee's oral communication. During the preconference session, the mentee may indicate an area in need of feedback which pertains to his or her oral communication skills. As the mentor observes the lesson, he or she writes down exactly what is said by the teacher, word for word, within this particular category. (If an observation requires that lengthy data be recorded, the use of shorthand or a tape recorder may be necessary.) During the postconference session, the information collected is analyzed and, if necessary, a plan for improving this area is formulated.

How Can I Use Word for Word?

There are many situations in which Word for Word would be an appropriate observation technique. Table 3-1 offers some suggestions for using Word for Word. Additional uses, specific to your situation, may be added to the list. (See Appendix A for a sample form to use with Word for Word.)

Table 3-1. Suggestions for Using Word for Word

- Giving directions
- Asking higher order questions
- Praising students
- Managing student behavior
- Using age-appropriate vocabulary
- Feedback for students with special needs
- Feedback for students of both genders
- Controlling voice dysfluencies (e.g., use of *um*)
- Word for Word outside the classroom
- _____
- _____
- _____

In addition to targeting areas of concern, Word for Word can also be used to highlight the mentee's strengths and to gather data as evidence of meeting professional teaching standards (see chapter 8).

Giving Directions

Giving directions in a clear and effective manner takes practice. New teachers may struggle with this particular area of communication. They may give directions that are too vague and then need to regain students' attention to clarify the directions. On the other hand, a new teacher may give several sets of directions at one time, and students may be overwhelmed by the information. Giving directions will also vary depending on the student(s) as well as the difficulty of the task.

Word for Word is an appropriate observation technique to provide feedback in this area. During the observed lesson, you write down what the mentee says, exactly as spoken, each time he or she gives directions. Then, at the postconference, the two of you would examine the data to identify the strengths and weaknesses in the mentee's ability to give directions and perhaps set goals for strengthening this skill.

Asking Higher Order Questions

Asking questions at various levels can be an area of difficulty for new teachers. Most have learned about the different cognitive levels of questions, such as those in Bloom's taxonomy (Bloom, Englehart, Furst, Hill, & Krathwohl, 1956). However, when faced with asking questions in their own classroom on a daily basis, they may limit questions to pure factual recall, which in turn limits students' responses and engagement.

By using Word for Word, the mentor can provide feedback on this important skill. While observing a lesson, the mentor would write down exactly what the teacher says each time he or she asks a question. The results can then be compared to Bloom's taxonomy (see Table 3-2), or another measure chosen by the mentor and mentee, to determine the type and variety of questions used by the new teacher.

Table 3-2. Bloom's Taxonomy for the Cognitive Domain

- Knowledge — recalling facts.
- Comprehension — restating the information into your own words.
- Application — applying the knowledge to new situations.
- Analysis — breaking down the information into parts.
- Synthesis — reorganizing the parts into something new.
- Evaluation — making judgments about the new information.

Praising Students

Praise can be quite reinforcing and motivating to students if it is used effectively, but providing effective praise can be challenging for even an experienced teacher. Good & Brophy (2000) state that the effectiveness of praise is in its *quality* rather than its *frequency*. They recommend that praise be directed toward students' efforts and accomplishments instead of being used as a tool for controlling or manipulating students. They also suggest that praise be simple, direct, genuine, and specific.

In addition to the suggestions above, there may be other elements of effective praise relevant to your mentee's philosophy. Word for Word can offer insight into a new teacher's use of praise in light of his or her beliefs about praise. By recording the mentee's attempts at praising students, both mentor and mentee have concrete, factual information to reflect upon afterward. The mentor can then present possible actions for improving this area or can give the new teacher simple, direct, genuine, and specific praise for his or her efforts in this area.

Managing Student Behavior

Classroom management is a common concern for beginning teachers. They may find it difficult to maintain a balance of lessons that are motivating and interactive within an environment that is manageable and conducive to learning. Times of transition may also pose a management problem. New teachers may find themselves resorting to negative language rather than positive language in their attempt to manage the classroom.

In each of the examples described above, as well as others that may pertain to your own situation, Word for Word can be an appropriate observation technique. For example, managing cooperative learning groups may be an area of concern for your mentee. Perhaps the actual lesson goes quite well, but when it is time to proceed to the next activity, the teacher feels unable to make a smooth transition. In this case, the mentor could observe a lesson with cooperative learning and script the teacher's speech during the transition times. This data may lead the mentor and mentee to identify where the problem lies; they can then proceed to developing strategies to improve the situation.

Using Age-Appropriate Vocabulary

"I would like to welcome," the first grade teacher begins, "John's mom as our *distinct* guest speaker." "My mom doesn't stink," defends John. If teachers have difficulty using age-appropriate vocabulary, a host of problems can result, from simple misunderstandings to more serious miscommunications. New teachers, especially, may not have had the experience or developed the skills for adjusting their vocabulary to meet the needs of their audience.

If using age-appropriate vocabulary is a concern for a mentee, Word for Word is a useful observation technique. By recording the mentee's exact words during a lesson, patterns linking teacher vocabulary choice to student misunderstandings may emerge. The new teacher may struggle with appropriate word choice in a variety of situations, such as presenting information, giving directions, asking questions, and clarifying information. In any of these instances, the mentor could suggest possible strategies, from which the mentee could select, to improve the communication between teacher and students in the mentee's classroom.

Feedback for Students With Special Needs

The Individuals with Disabilities Education Act (IDEA) has made it a common occurrence for school systems to have inclusive classrooms. More and more students with special needs are being educated with their peers in the general education classroom. This can sometimes pose a challenge for new teachers, especially those with no experience or training in special education. It is important that students with special needs are held to the same standards as their nondisabled peers, although they sometimes go about accomplishing those standards in unique ways.

Word for Word can be used to gather data in this area. It is possible for a new teacher to think that he or she is "talking down" to the students with special needs in the room or "watering down" his or her language. It is also possible that the teacher's feedback to students with special needs is more superficial than it is for the others. When a student with special needs answers a question incorrectly, how does the teacher respond? If the teacher responds negatively, chances are that the student will not contribute an answer next time. Another possibility for gathering data on feedback for students with special needs is to pair it with one of the other strategies already discussed. For example, is the teacher asking students with special needs all literal-level questions and leaving the higher order questions for the other students? The possibilities for data gathering are limited only by the decisions of the mentor and mentee.

Feedback for Students of Both Genders

Do I respond differently to boys than to girls? Do I respond more positively, or more often, to one or the other? These may be questions that concern your mentee. Although teachers strive to achieve equity in their feedback, they may unknowingly interact differently with students depending on their gender. Their feedback may differ in frequency as well as quality, and that feedback may change depending on the situation.

Results obtained from using Word for Word can provide mentor and mentee with some issues to consider. In addition to tallying the frequency of interactions with students of each gender, the mentor can script the kind of feedback the new teacher offers. Does the feedback change in relation to asking questions, praising, or disciplining? Is there a relationship between subject matter and the teacher's interactions with boys compared to girls? As with providing feedback for students with special needs, this area may be paired with other suggested uses of Word for Word presented in this chapter and may require some ongoing observations.

Controlling Voice Dysfluencies

We all, um, you know, do it from time to time. Controlling voice dysfluencies can be a challenge for many teachers, new and experienced alike. There may be different reasons for the cause, such as unfamiliarity with the content, nerves, or habit, and we may even be unaware that the situation exists.

The first step in improving this area of communication is to examine the frequency and circumstances surrounding its use. Perhaps there is a pattern as to when the voice dysfluencies occur most. Is it while retrieving information to share with the students or while disciplining? What seems to be the antecedent for the voice dysfluency in each case? Word for Word is a perfect observation technique to provide this kind of information. First, the mentor gathers data by recording the mentee's exact words during specific times in the lesson; the mentor may also note observations regarding the circumstances. Then the two can work together in determining the reason for such dysfluencies as well as approaches for improvement.

Word for Word Outside the Classroom

Rosenberg, O'Shea, & O'Shea (1998) list 11 important strategies that master teachers use with families. The first is implementing effective communication and interaction skills. Another strategy is planning and conducting collaborative conferences. New teachers often feel anxious about their first parent-teacher conferences. Acquiring the necessary skills to work with families provides an excellent opportunity for the mentee and the mentor to switch roles in the use of Word for Word. The new teacher should have the opportunity to observe his or her mentor's skills in working with families. This can be accomplished by asking the new teacher to sit in on a conference with the parents' permission, or the mentor can set up a role-playing situation for the observation to take place. Word for Word can be used to gather information about the mentor's use of positive language, questioning, clarifying, providing explanations, avoiding educational jargon, describing student work or behavior, and so forth. "By observing how effective teachers problem solve and work toward mutually agreed-on goals with students' families and by imitating experienced peers, new teachers can demonstrate the master teaching process" (p. 375).

Another place outside the classroom that Word for Word can be useful is in a special education team meeting. If the new teacher is a special educator who is responsible for presenting assessment findings at a team meeting, he or she may have difficulty clearly expressing the results to parents or answering parents' questions constructively. If the new teacher identifies this as an area of concern, the mentor might be invited to observe at a team meeting (given parental permission) and then analyze the results of the Word for Word data collection with the mentee before sharing suggestions.

Word for Word in Action

Only one month into her first year of teaching second grade, Sandy was asked by her principal to formulate three goals for the upcoming year. Sandy had a difficult time selecting only three goals because she wanted to do so much; her enthusiasm was unyielding. Finally, she decided that she really wanted her students to be critical thinkers, and one way she could help to foster that skill would be to include higher order questions in her lessons. She remembered a lesson she had done in her student teaching in which she asked the students questions covering all levels of Bloom's taxonomy. She was quite impressed with the amount of conversation and dialogue that came about as a result of the evaluation and analysis questions. So she made this one of her top priority goals for the year.

Sandy knew that since questioning was one of her goals for the year, she would be evaluated by the principal according to that goal in June. In order to prepare herself and to do an excellent job stimulating her students' thinking skills, she enlisted the help of her mentor. She spoke to the mentor about her goal at one of their regularly scheduled meetings, and they set up a time for the mentor to observe Sandy in action. When the day came, the mentor met with Sandy during a preconference and together they decided that the best way to collect data about Sandy's question levels would be to use Word for Word. The mentor also reminded Sandy that it was not her job to evaluate, but to collect information that they could review together, and then support Sandy in any changes she wanted to make.

Sandy's lesson was a shared book experience (Tierney & Readence, 2000), and she asked questions as the class went through the story together. Every time Sandy would ask a question, the mentor would write down, word for word, what she said. Later, during the postconference session, the two educators looked at the questions and labeled each one according to Bloom's taxonomy. Then Sandy talked about how she noticed, after looking at her own questions, that she had the highest number of questions at the knowledge and comprehension level. She remarked how surprised she was that the students were giving her one- and two-word answers, and now she knew why.

After some discussion, the mentor and Sandy came up with a list of action steps to help Sandy accomplish her goal. Sandy thought about each one and then decided on the action step that would best match her teaching style. The mentor gave her a sheet to clip in her plan book of suggested verbs to use when developing questions at the different levels of the taxonomy. Sandy also thought she needed to write out questions ahead of time when she was preparing her lessons until she became comfortable enough thinking of higher order questions "on her feet." In another month or so, the mentor and Sandy will collect further information on this goal and assess the progress made.

Questions for Collaborative Reflection

Teaching is an occupation that demands a lot of time, patience, and energy. Sometimes teachers get caught up in the daily routines and forget to take time to reflect on their classroom practices. Veteran teachers as well as new teachers need time for personal reflection as well as collaborative reflection with their colleagues. The following questions are meant to guide you as you work together with your mentee to improve classroom instruction. The questions can be reflected upon individually, or certain questions can be the trigger for collaborative reflection and sharing of thoughts and ideas. You or your mentee might feel more comfortable writing reactions to these questions in a personal or dialogue journal.

For the mentor:

- Have I made a collaborative effort to review and analyze the data collected using the Word for Word observation strategy?
- Did I meaningfully contribute ideas to the collaborative discussion of how to improve the specific area my mentee is working on?
- How can I use Word for Word to gather data on my own instructional language?
- In what other areas might Word for Word work as an observation strategy (add to Table 3-1)?

For the mentee:

- How was the use of Word for Word helpful in providing feedback about the area I targeted as a concern?
- Out of the list of suggestions my mentor and I constructed, which best suits my teaching style?
- What are my next immediate action steps to improve my teaching, based on the data gathered?
- What is my time line for revisiting this area and asking my mentor to do a follow-up observation?
- In what other areas might Word for Word work as an observation strategy (add to Table 3-1)?

References

Bloom, B., Englehart, M., Furst, E., Hill, W., Krathwohl, D. (Eds.). (1956). *Taxonomy of educational objectives: The classification of educational goals. Handbook I: Cognitive domain.* New York: Longmans Green.

Good, T. L., & Brophy, J. E. (2000). Management I: Preventing problems. In *Looking in classrooms* (8th ed., pp. 122–159). New York: Longman.

Rosenberg, M., O'Shea, L., & O'Shea, D. (1998). *Student teacher to master teacher: A practical guide for educating students with special needs* (2nd ed.). Upper Saddle River, NJ: Merrill.

Tierney, R. J., & Readence, E. K. (2000). *Reading strategies and practices: A compendium* (5th ed.). Needham Heights, MA: Allyn & Bacon.

4

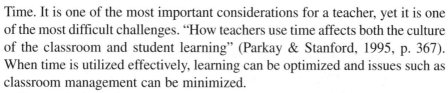

Observation Technique No. 2: Keeping Track of Time

Time. It is one of the most important considerations for a teacher, yet it is one of the most difficult challenges. "How teachers use time affects both the culture of the classroom and student learning" (Parkay & Stanford, 1995, p. 367). When time is utilized effectively, learning can be optimized and issues such as classroom management can be minimized.

Even experienced teachers continually strive to use time more efficiently. Therefore, it is not surprising that beginning teachers sometimes have difficulty with time management. Precious time may be lost during transitions and routines. New teachers may rush though some parts of a lesson or drag out other parts. Often they are left with time to fill or no time to finish what they planned. Collecting data to help a new teacher with time management skills is easy to do.

What Is Keeping Track of Time?

Keeping Track of Time is an observation technique that is useful when observing and collecting data based on the mentee's use of time. During the preconference session, the mentee may request guidance with his or her time management skills. As the mentor observes the lesson, he or she simply uses a stopwatch or clock to record how much time the teacher spends on a specific part or on various parts of the instruction. During the postconference, the teacher and mentor can search through the data and see where he or she is falling behind or spending too much unnecessary time. Then, if necessary, a plan for improving this area can be developed.

How Can I Use Keeping Track of Time?

There are many situations in which Keeping Track of Time would be an appropriate observation technique. Table 4-1 offers some suggestions for using Keeping Track of Time. Additional uses, specific to your situation, may be added to the list.

Table 4-1. Suggestions for Using Keeping Track of Time

- Transitions
- Morning routine, dismissal routine
- Lecturing
- Hands-on activities
- Wait time for student responses
- Maintaining attention and appropriate student behavior
- Giving and clarifying directions
- Meaningful reading and writing
- _____
- _____
- _____

In addition to using Keeping Track of Time to target areas of concern, it can also be used to highlight the mentee's strengths and to gather data as evidence of meeting professional teaching standards (see chapter 8).

Transitions

The bell rings to signal the start of second period, and most students aren't even in their seats yet. A few students are patiently waiting for class to begin, others are wandering to their seats ever so slowly, and a few more are hovering at the door offering their last words of advice to friends in the hall. In middle school and high school classrooms, the transitions from class to class can unnecessarily take up some valuable time for learning. Beginning teachers might find that it takes them a large amount of time to settle the students and begin class. Sometimes beginning teachers are overwhelmed by the schedule, and they find it difficult to be prepared when the next group of students walks into the room. If the teacher is unprepared to begin when the bell rings, more time is lost. Keeping Track of Time can provide documentation in this area.

The majority of classrooms today have many activity shifts that require students to move about within the classroom. Students often transition into cooperative groups, switch materials or resources needed for subject areas, and move through center-based learning activities. Varying activities is highly valuable for students' learning, but the time needed for transitions can be time taken from academic instruction if it's not done efficiently.

A mentor can use Keeping Track of Time to provide the beginning teacher with data that shows exactly how much time is being lost in transitions. Eventually, the beginning teacher can personally chart his or her time used during transitions to see if any progress is being made. Using this technique also provides the opportunity for the mentor and mentee to discuss routines and schedules that are so important for fluid transitions. "To facilitate efficient transitions, teachers need to arrange the physical environment appropriately, establish and enforce rules that encourage smooth transitions, and use signals to clearly indicate that activity shifts are going to occur" (Rosenberg, O'Shea, & O'Shea, 1998, p. 71).

Morning Routine, Dismissal Routine

A typical morning routine in school consists of attendance, lunch count, homework collection, notes for the office, questions, unpacking backpacks, office announcements, and sometimes a song, poem recitation, or flag salute. It's amazing that this doesn't take teachers half the morning to complete, especially those working with young children. All of these activities can be done quickly and with little confusion if teachers establish routines that are consistent and can be performed independently by the students. New teachers may need help condensing these morning tasks and developing strategies for using the time resourcefully. Keeping Track of Time can help the new teacher compare the time spent in the morning before and after implementation of routines.

Dismissal is another time of day that can affect classroom time. In some instances, new teachers spend too much time preparing students for dismissal. If this is the case, the mentor can show it with data collected from this technique and then share his or her own tips on how to ready the students for dismissal within a reasonable amount of time.

In other cases, new teachers find themselves rushing students out the door after teaching right up until the dismissal bell rings. In this case, students are often unorganized, the classroom is left untidy, and homework is forgotten in the desk. The mentor can keep track of time during the last period of the day and then confer with the mentee about setting up a schedule that would allow a sufficient amount of time for students to be dismissed without detracting too much from instructional time.

Lecturing

1:00 p.m.: "I'm going to ask you to take notes for about 10 minutes. Thomas Jefferson was the third president of the United States."... 1:21 p.m.: "So, as you can see, Jefferson had many important roles in this country even before he became president." Beginning teachers may spend more class time lecturing than they had originally planned. Perhaps they don't even realize the amount of time devoted to teacher-talk within a class. Whether intentional or not, lecturing can become the prevalent method of instruction. Lecturing, when used effectively, can be a useful format for presenting information. "A good lecture is systematic and sequential and conveys information in an orderly and interesting way" (Saphier & Gower, 1997, p. 283). The challenge is to balance lecture with other instructional methods to engage the students. (Videotaping may offer further insight into student behavior during lecture time. See chapter 7 for use of this technique.)

Keeping Track of Time can provide useful feedback to a new teacher on the time allotted in a lesson to lecturing. While observing, the mentor can record how much time is spent using the lecture format. Then, in the postconference, the mentor and mentee can examine the data to determine the balance of lecturing with other methods of instruction. This may also be an appropriate time for the two teachers to brainstorm alternatives to lecturing. In this way, the new teacher becomes aware of the time that he or she spends talking as well as the options for varying the presentation of information.

Hands-on Activities

Even back in the early 1900s, John Dewey (1956/1990) realized that it was quite natural for children to be intensely active. He saw that activity as something vital to the learning that takes place in school, not something to be diminished. It is through the active inquiry of a child that teaching can begin. Children need to be doing, not just listening, in order to understand. Dewey was clear that the child's instincts and activity are to be guided by the teacher.

Using hands-on materials and activities in the classroom captures the students' attention and allows each child to be an active part of the learning experience rather than a passive receiver. So, why would a mentor need to use a technique like Keeping Track of Time in this area?

Keeping Track of Time can be used to document how much time is spent on hands-on activities versus other related tasks (e.g., reading from a textbook, completing worksheets, listening, independent seat work). Reviewing this sort of data can help the new teacher to find a balance in classroom methods. It can also be used positively to document the new teacher's success with the smooth incorporation of activities that meaningfully represent the subject under study.

On the other hand, during a conference the new teacher might relay a concern that he or she is spending so much time on activities that the content is suffering. This technique can help the mentor and mentee to determine if an excessive amount of time is spent on activities that are not advancing students' learning.

Wait Time for Student Responses

What if someone asked you a question, and then gave you less than 1 second to respond? Time's up, what's your answer? Unfortunately, some research has shown that teachers, on average, wait less than 1 second for student responses (Rowe, 1986). However, significant benefits can result when wait time is increased. Rowe has reported the effects for both teachers and students. When wait time was increased, the number of questions a teacher asked decreased, but the quality of the questions increased. For students, both the number offering responses and the quality of the responses increased. It has also been found that interaction among students may improve as well. In essence, the "sound of silence" can be a powerful teaching tool.

Keeping Track of Time is the perfect technique for collecting data on a mentee's wait time. New teachers may be curious about their use of wait time, or they may express concern about the number and/or kind of answers their students have been offering. The mentor, then, can observe a lesson and document the teacher's use of wait time. The data collected from the lesson provides a basis for discussion and reflection between mentor and mentee. How long does the mentee allow for student responses? Does it appear that the wait time was sufficient? How might the mentee be reminded to use an appropriate wait time? As a follow-up, a combination of observation techniques, such as Keeping Track of Time and Word for Word (see chapter 3), can be used to measure progress in wait time and the quality of teacher questions and student responses.

Maintaining Attention and Appropriate Student Behavior

"Misbehavior is the most difficult problem teachers have to contend with. It is a problem because it interferes with teaching and learning, shortchanges students, and comes close to driving teachers nuts" (Charles, 2000, p. 6). Maintaining students' attention during a lesson or managing students' behaviors can be a real challenge to all teachers, but especially for a novice. Some inappropriate behaviors during a lesson are serious and need to be handled immediately. Other behaviors are minor and can be handled with nonverbal cues, proximity control, or attention signals. However, the beginning teacher may feel that he or she is spending too much time stopping and waiting for students' attention or commenting on particular students' behaviors throughout the lesson. Every time the teacher stops during a lesson, students can lose their thoughts or shift their attention away from the lesson. Keeping Track of Time allows the mentor to tally how many times the teacher stopped to manage behavior or attention, plus how long each interruption lasted. Later, the mentor might share resources or ideas about unobtrusive classroom management techniques.

Giving and Clarifying Directions

The ability to give clear directions is an acquired skill. Time spent on giving and clarifying directions may be a concern, especially for beginning teachers. They may spend a relatively small amount of time giving directions for a task and then realize that an enormous amount of time is spent clarifying the directions during the task. In this case, the teacher not only has to interrupt the students as they are engaged in the assignment but also may not have all the students' full attention. In another scenario, a new teacher may spend a lot of time giving directions for several tasks all at once, just to find that students are not able to remember the series of instructions. In both cases, time may be unnecessarily wasted.

If your mentee voices concern with the time consumed by giving and clarifying directions, Keeping Track of Time is an appropriate observation technique. Simply track the amount of time the mentee uses in this area during a scheduled observation, and then analyze the results together. An action plan for improving direction-giving may surface from the postconference session. For example, the mentee may decide to write out directions when planning for a lesson, or the mentee may try giving directions using a variety of modes: visually, verbally, or through active demonstration.

Meaningful Reading and Writing

The amount of time devoted to reading and writing varies from classroom to classroom. However, the amount of time devoted to *meaningful* reading and writing varies even more so. Furthermore, the discrepancy between the amount of time in school that higher achieving readers spend on actual reading in comparison to their lower achieving counterparts is quite astonishing, in some cases amounting to three times as much in a week's time (Allington, 2001). Although new teachers may allocate a good amount of time for literacy instruction, students may not be engaged in actual reading and writing for the majority of that time.

Keeping Track of Time can be used to measure meaningful reading and writing. In this situation, the mentor would keep a log of the time students spend on actual reading and/or writing during a class period (not on prereading activities, worksheets, writing answers to questions, or postreading activities). The information collected may support the existence of meaningful reading and writing, in which case the mentee can be assured of his or her efficient use of literacy time and perhaps monitor it on his or her own. On the other hand, if much time is being spent on peripheral activities, then the mentor and mentee can discuss the time spent on different parts of the lesson and how meaningful reading and writing time can be increased.

Keeping Track of Time in Action

After graduating with a double major in secondary education and physics, Sean took a job teaching eighth-grade science at a middle school near his hometown. Throughout the summer, Sean prepared his lessons and gathered resources that would support the curriculum he needed to cover during the academic year. The field of science absolutely fascinated Sean from the time he was very young, and he was eager to share that passion with his students.

September came and Sean was fully captivated by his new teaching responsibilities. Sean and his mentor, who was also knowledgeable in science, had a lot in common. The year began smoothly, but by the time November rolled around Sean was beginning to feel pressured that he didn't have enough time in the classroom to engage the students in activities that would cement their understanding of new concepts. He wanted to use cooperative learning and even include some content area reading strategies, but he just seemed to always run out of time. Turning to his mentor, Sean asked for some feedback about time management in the classroom.

Before providing any advice, Sean's mentor needed to know where the time was being lost in the classroom. During the preconference for an observation, the mentor asked Sean to describe a typical day in the class; this gave the mentor a preliminary idea about where time might be misused. The two gentlemen decided that for this particular observation, the mentor would use the technique Keeping Track of Time. The observation took place the next day during Sean's third-period science class.

Sean had prepared a class on energy transformation and designed an activity to accompany the lesson. Knowing that Sean was concerned about the lack of time for students to engage in their activities, the mentor decided to keep track of the time spent on direct instructional methods and the time students spent on the labs. Here is a sample of the mentor's notes:

Time	Activity
10:15	The students arrive.
10:19	Students are settled in and Sean begins going over last night's homework.
10:29	Sean begins talking about energy and energy transformation.
10:49	Sean gives directions for the activity to be done in class.
10:51	The students begin working on the activity assignment in pairs.
10:59	Sean instructs the students to begin clean-to-up.
11:01	The bell signals the end of the class period.

During the postconference, Sean and the mentor analyzed how time was used during the class session by reviewing the data. Sean didn't realize that going over the homework takes up at least 10 minutes of the period. He also never imagined that he did most of the talking in the classroom for an extended period of time. In this lesson he was talking more than 30 minutes from the time that class began until the students started the activity.

After much discussion, the two educators compiled a list of action steps to help Sean establish more effective use of instructional time in his classroom. Sean decided that he would correct the homework in class only if students seemed to have trouble with the assignment or needed a review. He also resolved to shorten the length of his lectures on the content and to intersperse some information to the groups as they were engaged in the activity. Sean's mentor helped him to realize that students will make stronger connections to the content if they are using the new information to help them complete the class activity or to solve a problem that arises. When Sean is comfortable with this new routine, he will invite the mentor back to update his progress in Keeping Track of Time.

Questions for Collaborative Reflection

For the mentor:

- Have I made it a collaborative effort to review and analyze the data collected using the Keeping Track of Time observation strategy?
- Did I meaningfully contribute ideas to the collaborative discussion of how to improve the specific area my mentee is working on?
- Did I guide my mentee toward developing action steps that are aligned with his or her teaching philosophy?
- In what other areas might Keeping Track of Time work as an observation strategy (add to Table 4-1)?

For the mentee:

- How was the use of Keeping Track of Time helpful in providing feedback about the area I targeted as a concern?
- What is my time line for revisiting this area and asking my mentor to do a follow-up observation?
- Am I comfortable with the action steps created for achieving my goal? If not, what might I change?
- In what other areas might Keeping Track of Time work as an observation strategy (add to Table 4-1)?

References

Allington, R. L. (2001). *What really matters to struggling readers: Designing research-based programs.* New York: Longman.

Charles, C. M. (2000). *The synergetic classroom: Joyful teaching and gentle discipline.* New York: Longman.

Dewey, J. (1990). *The school and society: The child and curriculum.* Chicago: University of Chicago Press. (Original work published 1956)

Parkay, F. W., & Stanford, B. H. (1995). *Becoming a teacher* (3rd ed.). Boston: Allyn & Bacon.

Rosenberg, M., O'Shea, L., & O'Shea, D. (1998). *Student teacher to master teacher: A practical guide for educating students with special needs* (2nd ed.). Upper Saddle River, NJ: Merrill.

Rowe, M. B. (1986). Wait time: Slowing down may be a way of speeding up. *Journal of Teacher Education, 37* (1), 43–50.

Saphier, J., & Gower, R. (1997). *The skillful teacher: Building your teaching skills* (5th ed.). Acton, MA: Research for Better Teaching.

5

Observation Technique No. 3: Mapping the Classroom— Movement and Materials

Think about the amount of time spent within the four walls of the classroom. This physical environment can have a considerable impact on teachers and students alike. Yet teachers have the power to organize the classroom to optimize learning.

> Teachers are assigned rooms that they did not design to accommodate groups of students whom they did not select. In spite of these unfavorable conditions, many teachers maximize their resources and enhance their leaning environments by carefully and creatively arranging their classrooms (Cangelosi, 2000, p. 278)

Making the most of our classroom environment as well as the materials therein is challenging for all teachers, beginning and experienced. Reflecting on the "map" of our classroom, however, can make the space within those four walls fresh, innovative, and, more important, productive.

What Is Mapping the Classroom?

Mapping the Classroom is an observation technique that is useful when observing and collecting data on the presence and use of movement and materials in the classroom. The technique may be used during a formal observation or at an informal meeting. During a formal observation, the mentor can draw a diagram of the classroom and record information specific to the mentee's concerns—for example, teacher or student movement. In an informal sense, Mapping the Classroom can be used to survey the physical environment of the classroom for reasons such as accessibility of classroom materials and safety in the classroom.

How Can I Use Mapping the Classroom?

There are many situations in which Mapping the Classroom would be an appropriate observation technique. Table 5-1 offers some suggestions for using Mapping the Classroom. Additional uses, specific to your situation, may be added to the list.

Table 5-1. Suggestions for Using Mapping the Classroom

- Maintaining attention
- Teacher movement within the classroom
- Student movement within the classroom
- Monitoring group work
- Effective use of classroom space
- Accessibility of classroom materials
- Safety in the classroom
- _____
- _____
- _____

In addition to using Mapping the Classroom to target areas of concern, it can also be used to highlight the mentee's strengths and to gather data as evidence of meeting professional teaching standards (see chapter 8).

Maintaining Attention

A look, a matter-of-fact stroll past a student, a gentle touch on a student's desk: these are all examples of subtle ways that teachers use movement to maintain students' attention. The advantage of techniques such as these is obvious. They allow a teacher to indiscreetly redirect a student's attention without disrupting the other students and interrupting the lesson. Furthermore, the student is not directly singled out in front of his or her peers. In some instances, using movement to maintain attention is an appropriate approach for managing a classroom.

How, then, can Mapping the Classroom help new teachers to become aware of their moves to maintain attention? Let's suppose a mentee requests feedback in this area. Perhaps he or she is still uncomfortable with using such strategies or wants an objective opinion on the effectiveness of these approaches. Using a simple diagram of the classroom, the mentor can record what kind of attention moves were used, how many times attention moves were used, where in the classroom they occurred, and what happened as a result of the actions. The data provides a springboard for discussion between mentor and mentee. Suggestions for possible attention moves for different circumstances and different students may emerge as well.

Teacher Movement Within the Classroom

A first-year teacher is standing, all eyes fixed upon her, at the front of the room as her lesson begins. Halfway through the lesson she is still standing at the front of the room, but some of the students in the back have lost their focus and are doing other things. By the end of the lesson, the teacher is still positioned in the front of the room, and there sits a student in the back row who misunderstood the directions and has incorrectly completed half the assignment.

New teachers often appear rigid and fixed at the front of the room. Sometimes they feel awkward leaving their comfort zone in front of the blackboard or at their desk, where their necessary materials might be in view. Other times they are just so concentrated on the procedures of the lesson that they forget to move.

Teacher movement through the classroom can eliminate many potential problems in different areas. The teacher's movement through the room helps to discourage the possibility of losing students' attention or having students misbehave. More important, the teacher can monitor students' work and use the opportunity to informally assess whether students understand the content or skill being covered. Students who are struggling can be detected right away, and reteaching can take place. Teachers often recommend putting the students who need extra attention in the front of the room so that they can easily be monitored. Shouldn't we be giving all our students, regardless of where they sit, that extra attention?

Using the observation technique Mapping the Classroom can allow the mentor to trace on paper the teacher's movement through the room. It also affords the mentor and mentee an opportunity to discuss the benefits of moving among the students in the classroom. Finally, it can help both new and experienced teachers to review where their attention lies in the classroom.

Student Movement Within the Classroom

During the course of a schoolday, there are many times when students must move within the classroom. At transition times, such as exiting the classroom, students must move in an orderly way without causing a major distraction to one another or other classrooms. We may encourage student movement as part of a lesson—for example, when using an energizer or grouping strategy. It may also be necessary for students to move within the classroom to confer with the teacher or another student or to gather supplies. Regardless of the reason, student movement in the classroom is inevitable and, in many cases, encouraged.

If a mentee requests feedback about student movement within the classroom, Mapping the Classroom can be an appropriate technique. By drawing a simple diagram of the classroom, the mentor can trace the various movements of students during an observation period. Particular attention can be given to transition and classroom routines as well as to appropriate pathways within the classroom. Furthermore, a discussion of techniques to incorporate productive student movement during lessons may emerge.

Monitoring Group Work

We all know the benefits of cooperative learning: improving social skills, increasing learning, promoting discussion and language, encouraging problem solving, and many others. Brain researchers tell us that working in groups in which we feel valued stimulates our brains to release neurotransmitters for pleasure, which in turn helps us to enjoy our work more (Jensen, 1998). Cunningham and Allington (1999) note the benefits for struggling readers when placed in cooperative groups. Many experienced teachers know the value of cooperative learning simply from their own experiences with it in the classroom.

After numerous teacher preparation courses and work in the schools, most new teachers feel fairly comfortable incorporating cooperative learning into their lessons. The challenge becomes how to monitor and manage the cooperative groups.

> One of the most valuable "teacher rules" for effective collaborative group learning is that the teacher's time when groups are working should not be used to grade papers, plan other instruction, leave the room, or do any of the myriad paperwork or other tasks that you have to do. (Ruddell, 2001, p. 392)

As groups are working, it's important that the teacher visits each group to monitor its progress, watch the group dynamics, and solve any disputes or problems that cannot be resolved by the group members. Sometimes new teachers, without realizing it, gravitate toward certain groups and avoid others. They might feel that certain groups will need more guidance or that other groups will need very little. However, it's important that the teacher visit all groups consistently. Regardless of level, all groups will welcome feedback from the teacher. In addition, while some groups may need the teacher's guidance with the task, other groups may need the teacher to challenge them with a higher level assignment if they finish early.

A mentor can use Mapping the Classroom to trace the mentee's movement among the groups in a lesson. Using a diagram of the classroom, the mentor should mark a tally beside each specific group whenever the teacher visits them. Later, the tally marks can be compared to analyze whether the teacher monitored all groups as needed. This technique can also be used in conjunction with Keeping Track of Time (see chapter 4), and the mentor can record how much time the teacher spent at each group.

Effective Use of Classroom Space

Classroom space, or lack thereof, can be one of the most frustrating aspects of teaching. As preservice teachers, we probably all dreamed about what our first classroom would be like: perhaps a reading corner and a listening center in an elementary classroom or computer and laboratory stations in a secondary classroom. Beyond the teacher's needs and wants, the students are also affected by the classroom space. "The way things are arranged in space makes a difference in how people function" (Saphier & Gower, 1997, p. 49). Although we cannot control the size of a classroom, we can control how effectively we utilize a classroom space.

Mapping the Classroom can be used to assess the use of classroom space. By drawing a diagram of the classroom, mentor and mentee can examine the layout. This map can spark discussion about possible alternatives to organizing the classroom space. The mentee may offer particular areas of need or concern. Considerations may include: placement of the teacher's and students' desks, use of furniture to create "sections," storage options for teacher and student supplies and materials, and varying the space used for different instructional purposes. If we improve the effectiveness of classroom space, we improve the potential for efficient learning opportunities.

Accessibility of Classroom Materials

Classroom materials serve many purposes; for example, they may support our instruction, enrich our teaching, and motivate our students. However, *where* we keep our materials is equally as important as *what* materials we have to offer. If students do not have access to necessary materials, such as paper and writing instruments, it can cause a disruption in the class as these students seek assistance from the teacher or from others. On the other hand, if students do not have access to supplementary materials, such as independent reading books and math manipulatives, they may never seek them out at all.

Mentor and mentee can use Mapping the Classroom to determine the location of both required and supportive materials. They can diagram the classroom, indicating the position of various materials, and use the data to discuss the strengths in access as well as options for improving access. Are pertinent materials easily accessible to students? Is there a system for renewing these materials when the supply dwindles? Do students know where they can find supplementary materials? Are supplies reasonably visible and accessible? In the design of a productive classroom environment, accessibility of materials is a valid concern.

Safety in the Classroom

As new teachers, many of us probably tripped over far too many student backpacks in the aisles of the classroom before establishing rules about where they could be kept. Safety for students is a top priority in teachers' classrooms and schools. Every teacher fears the day that a student might be injured in his or her classroom. Although teachers, new and experienced, try adamantly to create a safe classroom environment, sometimes there are possible hidden dangers that exist.

Mapping the Classroom can be useful to both mentor and mentee in evaluating the possible dangers that might be present in each other's classrooms. Draw a diagram of the classroom and mark with a colored pen the potential hazards that require attention. When evaluating the classroom, look for blocked fire exits, misplaced or broken furniture, glass items that could break and lead to injury, blocked aisles, access to sharp tools like the teacher's scissors, cleaning solutions, and heavy objects that could fall. There are many hazards that we sometimes don't see until it's too late. Especially in the early grades, it is imperative that teachers think about safety all day, every day.

Mapping the Classroom in Action

The shrill sound of the bell signaled the end of another day in third grade. The students began searching for their homework pads and piling the books and papers they needed on their desktops. Despite numerous teacher warnings, Alyssa made a beeline to the back of the classroom to gather her backpack and jacket. As she ran, she tripped on her untied shoelace and fell to the floor with a thud. The teacher's mouth fell open as she scrambled to Alyssa to see if she was all right. A student shouted, "She's bleeding!" One student called the nurse's office from the classroom phone, and the others lined up at the door so they could walk out to the buses with another teacher.

The nurse arrived with a wheelchair and took Alyssa down to her office, where they waited for her parents to arrive. Overcome with worry about her student, the teacher went back to the room to analyze what had happened. How could Alyssa have cut herself so bad when she fell onto a linoleum floor? What caused the cut on Alyssa's head?

After some investigating it became apparent that Alyssa's head had grazed the hinges of an easel that stood in the back of the room, where she fell. The easel was large and sturdy, but its brass hinges were sharp and protruding. The teacher had never noticed. The easel was placed in that particular spot because that's where the class met for its morning meeting every day. Now that she looked carefully, the teacher noticed that the easel was right in the line of student movement from their desks to the coat racks. What else might be a potential hazard, the teacher wondered.

The next time she met with her mentor, she relayed her concerns about classroom safety. The mentor and the teacher sat together and mapped out the classroom, discussing potential problem areas and the location of items such as furniture and materials that were in need of repair. They then mapped out a new layout for the classroom that eliminated some of the trouble areas.

Luckily, Alyssa's injuries were not serious. She vowed never to run in the classroom again and to always make sure that her shoes were tied.

Questions for Collaborative Reflection

For the mentor:

- Have I made a collaborative effort to review and analyze the data collected using the Mapping the Classroom observation strategy?
- Did I meaningfully contribute ideas to the collaborative discussion of how to improve the specific area my mentee is working on?
- Did I guide my mentee toward developing action steps that are aligned with his or her teaching philosophy?
- In what other areas might Mapping the Classroom work as an observation strategy (add to Table 5-1)?

For the mentee:

- How was the use of Mapping the Classroom helpful in providing feedback about the area I targeted as a concern?
- What is my time line for revisiting this area and asking my mentor to do a follow-up observation?
- Am I comfortable with the action steps created for achieving my goal? If not, what might I change?
- In what other areas might Mapping the Classroom work as an observation strategy (add to Table 5-1)?

References

Cangelosi, J. S. (2000). *Classroom management strategies: Gaining and maintaining students' cooperation* (4th ed.). New York: Wiley.

Cunningham, P. M., & Allington, R. L. (1999). *Classrooms that work: They can all read and write* (2nd ed.). New York: Longman.

Jensen, E. (1998). *Teaching with the brain in mind.* Alexandria, VA: Association for Supervision and Curriculum Development.

Ruddell, M. R. (2001). *Teaching content reading and writing* (3rd ed.). New York: Wiley.

Saphier, J., & Gower, R. (1997). *The skillful teacher: Building your teaching skills* (5th ed.). Acton, MA: Research for Better Teaching.

6

Observation Technique No. 4: Measuring Methodology

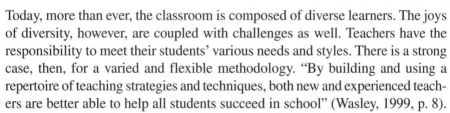

Today, more than ever, the classroom is composed of diverse learners. The joys of diversity, however, are coupled with challenges as well. Teachers have the responsibility to meet their students' various needs and styles. There is a strong case, then, for a varied and flexible methodology. "By building and using a repertoire of teaching strategies and techniques, both new and experienced teachers are better able to help all students succeed in school" (Wasley, 1999, p. 8).

Varying methodology alone is not enough, though; we have to *measure* our methodology: How effective is this set of instructional strategies? With what grouping methods are my students most productive? Did this assessment method provide the information I had intended? What classroom management methods seem to be most effective? To answer questions such as these, we need to move beyond simply planning to vary our methods toward reflecting upon our choices.

What Is Measuring Methodology?

Measuring Methodology is appropriate for examining a teacher's methodology. The information provided by this technique can help teachers not only to review their variety of methods but also to reflect on the effectiveness of these methods.

Measuring Methodology can be both an observation checklist and a self-assessment tool. Appendix B is an example of a Measuring Methodology Matrix for mentors to use during an observation. Depending on the needs of the mentee, it can be used to record the variety of methods employed during one observation, or it can be used in subsequent observations as well to provide ongoing data for collaborative reflection and analysis. Appendix C is an example of a Measuring Methodology Matrix intended for mentee self-assessment. This matrix can be used by the mentee to chart his or her own growth in this area.

How Can I Use Measuring Methodology?

There are many situations in which Measuring Methodology would be an appropriate observation technique. Table 6-1 offers some suggestions for using Measuring Methodology. Additional uses, specific to your situation, may be added to the list.

Table 6-1. Suggestions for Using Measuring Methodology

- Instructional methods

- Grouping methods

- Assessment methods

- Classroom management methods

- _____

- _____

- _____

In addition to using Measuring Methodology to target areas of concern, it can also be used to highlight the mentee's strengths and to gather data as evidence of meeting professional teaching standards (see chapter 8).

Instructional Methods

Chances are that when we consider the term *methodology*, we immediately think about our instructional methods, the *how* of teaching. Measuring Methodology can be used to examine the variety and effectiveness of a teacher's instructional methods. Within this realm of instruction, there are several methodological aspects to consider:

- Balance of methods
- Scaffolding instruction
- Use of technology
- Mode of presentation

Providing a balance of instructional methods helps teachers to meet the diverse needs of their students. Furthermore, novelty in instructional strategies keeps students motivated to learn, improves attention, and enriches learning (Jensen, 1998). Measuring Methodology can be an effective technique for examining the balance of methods employed by a mentee. If a mentee would like feedback in this area, a mentor could conduct an observation and chart the different methods employed by the mentee; for example, lecture, questions and answers, discussion, group work. The mentee may not even be aware of the variety of methods he or she utilizes. After the observation, the mentee can then rate the effectiveness of these methods, under the guidance of the mentor, and a plan of action can be developed for this area if necessary. The mentee can also chart his or her own use of methods, rated for effectiveness, for several weeks and then share those results with the mentor for appropriate feedback.

In addition to balancing various instructional methods, it is important to scaffold instruction, in which students are supported in their learning while moving toward eventual independence. To scaffold instruction, Pearson and Gallagher (1983) suggest the "gradual release of responsibility." In this model, the responsibility for task completion gradually shifts from teacher modeling to guided practice to independent practice or application. A mentee could apply this model to a particular concept or subject. The Measuring Methodology Matrix could then be used to chart the different types of methods employed at the various stages (modeling, guided practice, independent practice/application) as well as the effectiveness of these methods. In an observation situation, the mentor could combine recording the method(s) the mentee uses in each stage along with the time spent at each stage (see chapter 4). Either way, the information gathered from this technique can assist the new teacher in measuring his or her instructional scaffolding methods.

Another aspect of instructional methods to consider is the use of technology. Within this area, teachers need to determine appropriate and effective uses of technology:

> Perhaps one of the reasons technology isn't working as well or as efficiently as many had hoped by now is that too frequently technology is chosen for insufficient reasons…if technology is to improve, teachers must recognize the difference between a technology solution that makes a difference and one that is an inessential add-on. (Roblyer & Edwards, 2000, p. 40)

Measuring methodology can assist a new teacher in examining the effectiveness of technology integration. When reflecting on technology use, you may want to consider variety, authenticity, and interactivity. Computers, for example, can offer an array of possibilities; varying the use will expand students' technological "literacy." On the other hand, it is important to incorporate authentic uses of technology to avoid the "inessential add-on" discussed above. Finally, experiences with technology should be interactive in nature. For example, when viewing a video, set a purpose for viewing and stop the tape periodically for discussion. Developing a video guide for students to follow as they view is another option. When integrated thoughtfully, technology has tremendous potential. A mentor can support his or her mentee in utilizing this resource.

A final consideration of instructional methods is mode of presentation. Most likely, if a teacher varies instructional methods, scaffolds instruction, and uses technology, his or her mode of presentation will be diversified. Measuring Methodology, however, can be used to gather data in this area. Through mentor observation or mentee self-assessment, a Measuring Methodology Matrix can be designed to chart the different modes utilized in presenting information along with the effectiveness ratings of these modes.

Grouping Methods

Cooperative learning has become a common occurrence in most classrooms today. Harris & Hodges (1995) define cooperative learning as "any pattern of classroom organization that allows students to work together to achieve their individual goals" (p. 45). In fact, research on cooperative learning has emphasized its benefits for students academically, socially, and attitudinally (Johnson & Johnson, 1994; Slavin, 1995). Although there is still a place for individual work in the classroom, there is a benefit to interspersing cooperative learning through various grouping methods.

By using Measuring Methodology, new and veteran teachers alike can keep a record of the different grouping methods exercised in their classrooms. During an observation or series of observations, the mentor could list the grouping methods employed by the mentee. The mentee could then rate the effectiveness of these strategies, and both mentor and mentee could discuss the results. Another option is using Measuring Methodology as a self-assessment tool in which the mentee tracks his or her own grouping methods with a mentor's guidance. The grouping methods listed on the Measuring Methodology matrix will depend on the individual teacher's style. They should include grouping strategies that the teacher is comfortable with as well as one or two new strategies to try to implement, perhaps a recommendation from the mentor.

Some possible grouping methods to think about include the following:

- Pairs (student choice)
- Pairs (teacher assigned)
- Triads (mixed or similar abilities)
- Small groups (mixed abilities)
- Small groups (similar abilities)
- Small groups (similar interests)
- Two large groups (class divided in half)
- Whole class

Many times it is necessary for the teacher to assign his or her students to pairs or small groups because of skill levels, personalities, or social issues. However, it is equally important that on occasion, we allow students to choose. Jensen's (1998) research on the brain and learning indicates that allowing students a choice (of partners, content, resources) will increase their intrinsic motivation and improve their attention for learning. Pairs, triads, or small groups can also be formed around students' interests. If the teacher is beginning a new unit—for example, studying a specific country—students might group to research a particular aspect of the country (e.g., resources, economics, traditions, food) depending on personal interests. Students can also be divided into two large groups for cooperative work; an example might be researching facts in preparing for a formal debate on an issue in history or another subject area.

In addition to tracking the grouping methods on the matrix, the new teacher should also identify his or her perception of how effectively each method was implemented. Grouping alone is not enough. The teacher needs to model for students how to work in groups; he or she has to practice the role of facilitator and needs to promote interdependence as well as individual responsibility in a group situation (Evertson, Emmer, & Worsham, 2000). To provide further data, this technique can be combined with the Sights and Sounds of the Classroom (see chapter 7). As the teacher becomes more and more proficient at his or her role, the more effective each of these grouping methods will become.

Assessment Methods

> Within the constraints of having in most settings too many students, and in the case of secondary teachers meeting the students each day in relatively short periods…it is important to find as many *different* ways as possible for students to share with you their understandings of the content under study. This is a constructive way of ensuring that students know you have high expectations for them and that your primary interest is helping them be successful learners. (Perrone, 1991, p. 60)

Too often in the past, teachers relied heavily on only one form of assessment. The students who were successful were probably the ones whose learning style was a match for that particular mode of assessment. With the increasing diversity and ability levels in our classrooms today, it is imperative that teachers take Perrone's advice and find *different* ways to measure students' knowledge, skills, and understandings.

If your mentee is concerned that he or she is frequently using only one type of assessment, then you might suggest using Measuring Methodology as a way to focus the new teacher on varying his or her assessment methods. Begin by listing on the matrix assessment types that the teacher already uses regularly. In many instances these might include quizzes, tests, papers, and student projects. Then add another form of assessment that the new teacher feels comfortable trying. Some other assessment methods include the following:

- Oral presentations
- Performance-based assessment
- Portfolio assessment
- Written assessments
- Teacher observation or anecdotal records

- Student self-assessment
- Student choice of assessment

As the mentor, you can introduce a few of these methods to your mentee and guide him or her through their implementation. If your mentee is interested in trying a new form of assessment, such as student portfolios, but is unsure about where to begin or what to include, you might suggest some professional development opportunities on that topic. As the mentee becomes comfortable with some of these other methods, he or she can add them to the matrix.

It is important to stress that the method of assessment should match the method of instruction. Make the new teacher aware that the type of assessment chosen to represent a student's learning should be relevant to what has been taught. It is much more relevant for a student learning to play an instrument to demonstrate his or her new skill by playing a piece of music rather than simply by identifying notes.

Another suggestion you might offer your mentee is to occasionally allow students the option to choose their own form of assessment. Let them individually choose how they want to show the teacher and others what they have learned. Ask the students to come up with a plan and present it for approval, or give the student a menu of options to choose from (be certain the options cover all learning styles). In this way, students capitalize on their strengths, which helps them to be successful.

Classroom Management Methods

Classroom management is probably the most challenging area new teachers deal with their first few years in the classroom. Regardless of the age group, learning best takes place in classrooms where the students feel safe, comfortable, and happy. That means a classroom that runs efficiently day to day, where students are attentive and engaged most of the time. Most likely your mentee has taken a course in classroom management through his or her teacher education program. He or she has probably been exposed to numerous classroom management techniques through the course and through observations and practicums in the schools. However, it can sometimes take a while before the teacher finds a method that is a good match for his or her style and for a particular group of students.

We believe that a teacher's choice of classroom management methods is closely tied to his or her educational philosophy. Therefore, it is not our intention to list the numerous methods but rather to explain how Measuring Methodology can work with whichever method your mentee chooses.

Unlike instructional methods, assessment methods, or grouping methods, classroom management techniques should not change frequently and should be consistently applied for as long as they are working effectively. Measuring Methodology can help you and your mentee to analyze and reflect upon a specific management method and its efficacy.

On the matrix, have your mentee list the classroom management method(s) that he or she is going to use. For example, a primary grade teacher might decide to use individual sticker charts to reward students for positive behaviors. A secondary teacher might implement peer conflict resolution in the classroom. In order to determine if the method is producing positive results, the teacher can rate the method after reflecting on the day's events. The teacher should maintain the matrix and the daily ratings for at least 4 to 6 weeks. By examining the ratings and comments on the matrix, the teacher can determine whether the method should be discontinued. If a method is initially rated as "ineffective" but gradually, over a few weeks, becomes "mostly effective," then the method is probably being applied consistently and is having a clear effect. On the other hand, if a method continues to be rated "ineffective" over a period of 4 weeks, it is probably best to revisit how it is being applied or to try something different. This is where your expertise as an experienced mentor teacher might be beneficial to your mentee.

Another way you can help your mentee to use Measuring Methodology is to keep track of individual student behavior plans, homework incentive plans, and so forth. Teachers sometimes make contracts with specific students on behavior or homework policies and need some way to keep track of the students' progress. One suggestion is to create a matrix for each student who has an individual, specific plan and to chart each day how the student is progressing on the plan and how effective the plan is for that particular student. By keeping the matrix close by, the teacher can rate the plan as well as comment on specific behaviors and events, both positive and negative. Later, the matrices for this student can serve as anecdotal records for use in planning for instruction, parent conferences, and/or Individualized Education Plan (IEP) meetings.

As the mentor, help your mentee to think carefully about how this observation technique can document his or her success with classroom management.

Measuring Methodology in Action

It was early September, and Mike was eager to begin his second year of teaching sixth-grade mathematics at his local middle school. The school had two instructional teams for each grade level; Mike was on one team, and his mentor, Brian, was on the other. Brian also taught mathematics and had been at this middle school for 12 years. He was instrumental in helping Mike make a smooth transition from student teaching into his first year in the classroom. Brian and the other teachers in the sixth grade knew that Mike was a "natural" teacher. He had in depth knowledge of the content and mathematics pedagogy. The students seemed to love his teaching style, and his first year administrative evaluations were outstanding. Now that the opening of his second year of teaching was quickly approaching, Mike began to think about how he could make this an even better year for his students and improve upon his teaching.

Although Brian was not Mike's "official" mentor this year, they still ate lunch together and met occasionally because they had become good friends. One of the areas Brian was always emphasizing as one of Mike's strengths was his varying methodology. The students enjoyed his class because it was never the same day in and day out. The methods varied, keeping the students interested in what they were learning. One day at lunch Mike mentioned that he was working on his professional portfolio. Brian urged him to document the varying methods he used in his class and include that as evidence in his portfolio. In order to document the varying methods, Brian gave Mike a blank copy of the Measuring Methodology Matrix and explained how to use it.

As a math teacher, Mike was familiar with the *Professional Standards for Teaching Mathematics* (National Council of Teachers of Mathematics, 1991), and he consulted them again to be certain that he included methods on his matrix that aligned with the standards. After thinking carefully about his students, his curriculum, and his teaching style, he put the following methods on his matrix: Problem Solving; Use of Representations (visual, concrete, graphic); Use of the District Math Text; Including Computer Software; Use of Calculators, Manipulatives, Math Aids; Student Engagement in Math Discourse; Modeling; Independent Practice; Application; Student Reflection (interpreting problems, defending results, describing problem-solving strategies).

Each week as he planned his lessons, he referred to the grid and checked off the various methods he would be using to teach a particular concept. (Appendix D shows a completed matrix for a week.) After a method was implemented, he reflected on how effective it was and how comfortable he felt using it. After a few weeks of collecting documentation, Mike noticed that he really did vary his methodology, and the only area he needed to address more often was that of including technology, such as the computer and specific software targeted to the concepts being taught. Now that he saw this as a need, he was prepared to investigate the most effective computer programs that might be purchased for the sixth graders. Mike felt that his implementation of most of the methods on the matrix was "mostly effective" except for student reflection, which he rated as being "somewhat effective" because he was still perfecting his own skills in that area.

Mike showed the matrices to Brian and thanked him for the idea. He told Brian that the process of referring to the matrix helped him to keep track of which methods he was relying on too much. If he didn't vary his methods somewhat, then he was probably not reaching all his students with different learning styles. The matrices went into his portfolio with a brief reflective narrative on their purpose and importance. Mike plans on keeping a copy of this matrix in the back of his plan book to use informally when planning lessons.

Questions for Collaborative Reflection

For the mentor:

- Do I vary my instructional methods, grouping methods, assessment methods?
- Which specific methods do I utilize under each of the categories above? Is there a method that my mentee uses that I might want to try and include in my own teaching?
- How can I help my mentee to become more proficient in the methods he or she identifies as implementing ineffectively?
- In what other areas might Measuring Methodology work as an observation strategy (add to Table 6-1)?

For the mentee:

- Do I need to use Measuring Methodology for my instructional methods, grouping methods, assessment methods, or classroom management methods? Choose one to target.
- In reviewing my completed grid, do I notice any methods that I have not implemented? Are there any methods I rely on too often?
- In thinking about the methods I rated as "ineffective," how comfortable was I in implementing those methods? Was it my first time trying the method? Is there a correlation between the ratings on my grid and my level of comfort with the different methods?
- In what other areas might Measuring Methodology work as an observation strategy (add to Table 6-1)?

References

Evertson, C., Emmer, E., & Worsham, M. E. (2000). *Classroom management for elementary teachers* (5th ed). Boston: Allyn & Bacon.

Harris, T. L., & Hodges, R. E. (Eds.). (1995). *The literacy dictionary: The vocabulary of reading and writing.* Newark, DE: International Reading Association.

Jensen, E. (1998). *Teaching with the brain in mind.* Alexandria, VA: Association for Supervision and Curriculum Development.

Johnson, D., & Johnson, R. (1994). *Learning together and alone: Cooperative, competitive, and individualistic learning* (4th ed). Boston: Allyn & Bacon.

National Council of Teachers of Mathematics. (1991). *Professional Standards for Teaching Mathematics.* Reston, VA: National Council of Teachers of Mathematics.

Pearson, P. D., & Gallagher, M. C. (1983). The instruction of reading comprehension. *Contemporary Educational Psychology, 8,* (3), 317–344.

Perrone, V. (1991). *A letter to teachers: Reflections on schooling and the art of teaching.* San Francisco, CA: Jossey-Bass.

Roblyer, M. D., & Edwards, J. (2000). *Intergrating educational technology into teaching* (2nd ed). Upper Saddle River, NJ: Merrill.

Slavin, R. E. (1995). *Cooperative learning: Research, theory, and practice* (2nd ed). Boston: Allyn & Bacon.

Wasley, P. (1999). Teaching worth celebrating. *Educational Leadership, 56* (8), 8–13.

Chapter

7

Observation Technique No. 5: The Sights and Sounds of the Classroom

Most of us would probably agree that it is awkward to see ourselves on video or hear ourselves on an audio recording, yet we must also admit that it can be enlightening. Although we are often our own toughest critic, these mediums can provide valuable information, particularly in a classroom environment.

Novice and seasoned teachers alike can profit from video- and audiotaping. At least one videotaped lesson is usually required of student teachers, and in a teacher education program, preservice teachers are sometimes required to audiotape a lesson. At the other end of the spectrum, the National Board for Professional Teaching Standards (NBPTS) has a rigorous program of standards and assessment for experienced teachers to earn National Board certification. One of the evidences that teachers gather in this process is videotapes of their teaching, which they in turn reflect upon and use to write a detailed analysis of their teaching.

As we can see, regardless of where a teacher stands on the continuum of experience, the sights and sounds of the classroom are worth investigating.

What Is the Sights and Sounds of the Classroom?

The Sights and Sounds of the Classroom is simply an observation technique that utilizes videotaping and/or audiotaping. A mentor could videotape or audiotape a lesson during a scheduled observation, or, in the interest of time, a mentee could videotape or audiotape a lesson for the mentor and mentee to collaboratively analyze afterwards. The benefit of video- and audiotaping is the opportunity to collect objective data on student behavior as well as teacher behavior. Furthermore, when utilizing audiotaping, the visual stimuli are not present, so it is easier to focus and concentrate only on the audio. Therefore, if oral communication is the identified area of concern, it's probably best to use an audiotape, which minimizes other distractions.

How Can I Use the
Sights and Sounds of the Classroom?

There are many situations in which the Sights and Sounds of the Classroom would be an appropriate observation technique. Table 7-1 offers some suggestions for using this technique. Additional uses, specific to your situation, may be added to the list.

In addition to targeting areas of concern, the Sights and Sounds of the Classroom can also be used to highlight the mentee's strengths and to gather data as evidence of meeting professional teaching standards (see chapter 8).

Table 7-1. Suggestions for Using the Sights and Sounds of the Classroom

The Sights of the Classroom

- Analyzing body language
- Tracking students' on-task and off-task behavior
- Examining routines and transition times
- Managing multiple small groups
- _____
- _____
- _____

The Sounds of the Classroom

- Controlling voice dysfluencies
- Speaking pace
- Using voice to maintain interest
- Using grammatically correct language
- Communicating directions clearly
- Analyzing a student's communication skills
- _____
- _____
- _____

The Sights of the Classroom

Analyzing Body Language

Body language is undoubtedly a powerful form of communication. Hand gestures, posture, stance, eye contact, and other forms of body language are all ways we send messages to our students. These messages can be positive and reinforcing, such as giving a thumbs-up when a student contributes a correct answer. Sometimes teachers establish body language signals with students ahead of time so that the students can be reminded to stay on task, refrain from talking, and so forth without being called upon frequently. However, body language can also send mixed messages or even negative messages to students. For example, a second-grade student eagerly approaches the teacher's desk, desperately wanting to share a story about what happened to him over the weekend. The student begins talking, and the teacher keeps his head down, glancing over the plans on his desk but nodding to the student at the same time. What message is this sending? Would the teacher allow the student to keep his head down, working on something else, while he was talking to him? Most of the time a teacher's body language is not intentional, and he or she is not even aware of the underlying messages being communicated. That's why analyzing and reflecting on one's teaching through videotape can be enlightening.

Tracking Students' On-Task and Off-Task Behavior

Unfortunately, teachers do not have "eyes in the back of their head," although we sometimes tease our students that we do. In a way, though, as teachers become more experienced, they can monitor a variety of tasks at one time. New teachers, on the other hand, may have difficulty keeping track of students' on-task and off-task behavior within the dynamics of an active classroom.

The benefit of videotaping is that it allows observation of student behavior as well as teacher behavior. There may be several instances when a mentee would want to examine students' behavior—for example, during a lecture or small-group work. If a lecture runs too long, it will be evident in students' behavior. A video will show if students' attention begins to wander. From an observer's standpoint in viewing the video, the mentee may identify these signals and better recognize them in future lessons. Similarly, when a teacher is working with a small group or all the students are working in cooperative groups, tracking students' on-task and off-task behavior can be a challenge. A video may provide insight of what works and what doesn't work in these classroom situations.

Examining Routines and Transition Times

In "Keeping Track of Time" (see chapter 4), we discussed recording time spent on routines and transitions in the classroom. If a new teacher is spending a considerable amount of time in one of these areas, the next step might be to videotape during a transition period. Viewing the video might help the mentee to locate the source of his or her problem with transitions or to think of ways to redesign routines. In the same fashion, the mentor might wish to videotape his or her classroom during transitions and give it to the new teacher to view. This might help to spark some new ideas for the teacher to try and allow the mentor an opportunity to watch and improve his or her own transition periods.

Managing Multiple Small Groups

"The teacher's role as students work in groups is a critical one. Whatever you do, don't be misled into thinking that once the groups are operational, your work is over. Far from it" (Ruddell, 2001, p. 392). Just as students need time and practice assuming their roles as a group member, a new teacher needs the same in assuming his or her role during group time. How do I attend to all the groups? How do I know if I have indeed attended to all the groups? How do I know if a group is on task? How do I know if all members of a group are participating and contributing to the process? These questions deal with both teacher and student behavior. Therefore, videotaping can be an appropriate observation technique.

If there is an abundance of questions and concerns about managing small groups, a new teacher may even avoid implementing this strategy. To encourage and support the use of small groups, a mentor could share a video of a group activity in his or her own classroom. Viewing this together, the mentor and mentee could develop a list of effective management strategies. Providing professional reading in this area could also supplement this list (see chapter 9). In another scenario, the mentor could videotape a lesson in which the mentee utilized small groups, or the mentee could videotape him- or herself to analyze with the mentor at their next meeting.

The Sounds of the Classroom

Controlling Voice Dysfluencies

Voice dysfluencies, such as constantly using the word *like* or interjecting an *um* now and then, are hard habits to break. Most often the person doesn't realize the frequency of his or her voice dysfluencies. In chapter 3 we discussed using the observation technique Word for Word to identify voice dysfluencies and their antecedents. Audiotaping can complement the data collected through other techniques. Hearing his or her own voice dysfluencies might bring the problem to a conscious level so that the new teacher can develop ways to reduce the occurrences.

Speaking Pace

Sometimes we are so nervous or perhaps we are excited or it may even be a habit but what can happen is that we can tend to speak too fast. On the other hand, sometimes . . . we . . . may . . . speak . . . at . . . a . . . very . . . slow . . . pace. Either way, our communication skills are compromised when our speaking pace is not optimal. Pace can be a particular concern for students with special needs and students for whom English is a second language. An audio-tape of a teacher's voice has no visual distractions; thus, it allows the listener to concentrate solely on an area of communication, such as speaking pace. In addition, an audiotape is an objective measure for a mentee to examine his or her own communication in this area rather than having a mentor judge what is or what is not an appropriate pace. Then, the mentor and mentee can devise an action plan together to strengthen this area.

Using Voice to Maintain Interest

Have you ever listened to a professional storyteller? The way a storyteller uses his or her voice helps to make the story come alive. Children are often en-tranced as they listen to the voices of the different characters or hear the storyteller's voice change pitch as the dramatic climax draws near. The same thing happens in many classrooms when teachers read aloud to their students. If the students had to listen to a drab, monotone voice throughout the book, they would probably lose interest. The use of voice is important not only when reading or telling stories but also throughout the day. A teacher's voice can signal when it's time to get serious and when it's time to have fun. Many teach-ers capture the attention of their talking students by whispering. When teaching content, teachers can emphasize important material by the intonation of their voices. Dramatic effects can be created through the use of voice, and it is these effects that will grab and maintain student attention. Audiotaping is a great way for the teacher to focus on his or her use of voice.

Using Grammatically Correct Language

Similar to controlling voice dysfluencies and speaking pace, using grammati-cally correct language can be a sensitive topic. Perhaps the best way for a mentor to provide feedback in this area is through the use of audiotaping. A new teacher may or may not be aware of incorrect grammar usage. If this area is identified as a concern by the mentee, then an audiotape can give evidence of the extent of the problem. If a new teacher does not specifically identify this area, he or she may become aware of the issue when reviewing audiotapes for a different purpose. Again, sometimes by simply recognizing the problem, a teacher may improve through a conscious effort.

Communicating Directions Clearly

"Communicating information and directions in a clear, comprehensible manner is an important teaching skill" (Evertson, Emmer, & Worsham, 2000, p. 103). New teachers are often so focused on the content they are teaching or the lesson and activity they have planned that they forget to work through the most important details, such as giving directions. In some instances, the teacher gives all the direc-tions at once orally, and students have trouble remembering the sequence of the directions. At other times, the teacher is so comfortable with the lesson or activity that he or she leaves out important steps in the directions. It is a sure sign of unclear directions if students are constantly asking questions about what to do next or are sitting there with blank expressions, not knowing what's expected of them. As the mentor, you can audiotape one of your mentee's lessons or have the mentee audio-tape on his or her own. Then, both of you can sit together and analyze the tape for evidence of clearly communicated directions. You might consider the following questions: How often were the directions repeated? Were the directions clarified and paraphrased for the students? Did the students have the opportunity to state the directions in their own words? How many times did the teacher have to stop the activity to restate the directions?

Analyzing a Student's Communication Skills

Although novice teachers often have concerns about their own teaching and communication skills, they tend to have numerous uncertainties about their students as well. For example, suppose a mentee identified a student who he or she thought had unidentified speech and/or language difficulties. It might be the first time that the new teacher has identified a possible problem in the area of speech and language. Maybe the new teacher is not sure whether he or she should ask the speech therapist to screen the child. The mentee asks the mentor for some help in deciding whether or not to pursue this issue with the school's speech therapist. As the mentor, you might suggest gaining parental permis-sion and audiotaping the child's language during a lesson. Then the tape can be reviewed by both of you, and a decision can be reached as to whether the speech therapist should also hear the tape to settle the question of whether the child should be screened.

You might also suggest that the new teacher audiotape each student in his or her class at least twice a year. Depending on the grade level, students can be taped reading, conducting presentations, engaged in group work, and so forth. Having these tapes to reflect upon will give the new teacher valuable informa-tion about the communication skills of his or her students and will also serve as documentation of student growth during the year.

The Sights and Sounds of the Classroom in Action

Caitlin was a first-year special education teacher. She was working with young children in the first grade who had mild disabilities. Caitlin's mentor, Mackenna, was another special educator in the same building who worked with the second graders. Caitlin was very skilled and knowledgeable; she seemed to have a natural gift for working with children with special needs. Caitlin spent most of her time in the general education inclusive classroom, supporting the students on her caseload. Sometimes she co-taught a lesson with the classroom teacher, at other times she made modifications and accommodations, and often she circulated about the room or sat by one of her students to provide assistance.

During college, Caitlin was an active student member of the Council for Exceptional Children (CEC). As part of that group, she became very familiar with the national organization and the services and supports it provides to students with exceptionalities as well as the teachers and parents who work with them. This year she was a professional member of CEC and had attended their conference earlier in the school year. Her portfolio was designed to address the core standards for beginning special educators that were developed by CEC. One of the standards she was addressing had to do with communication skills. She asked Mackenna how she might provide evidence of her effective communication skills in the portfolio, and her mentor suggested audiotaping.

During one of her sessions within the general education classroom, Caitlin kept a tape recorder by her and her student. She recorded approximately 20 minutes of her instruction with the first grader. After school that day, she met with Mackenna to review the tape.

Although Caitlin was very critical of herself, as most people are when listening to their own voices, Mackenna guided her to focus on some of the important things that happened during this taping. First of all, Caitlin spoke in a calm and soothing manner to this child, who can become easily agitated at times. She also spoke at a rate that was easy for the child to follow and understand. One of the most difficult tasks for a special educator is to provide instructional support in an inclusive classroom without disrupting the rest of the group or distracting attention from the general education teacher who is leading the lesson. Caitlin's volume was perfect; she was loud enough for her student to hear her without drawing others' attention from the lesson in progress. Another very important communication skill that Mackenna noticed throughout the tape was that whenever the classroom teacher gave directions or information to the class, Caitlin could be heard immediately afterward clarifying and simplifying the teacher's words for this particular student. In fact, sometimes she modified the instructions so that the student would be more successful with the activity. Knowing how vital this skill is in special education, Mackenna recommended that Caitlin script out portions of the tape and highlight the comparison between what the general education teacher could be heard saying and how Caitlin interpreted that information for her student.

Another benefit Caitlin found from using the tape was that she not only learned about her own communication skills, she also gained valuable information about this student. Having only to focus on listening, Caitlin realized that in the 20 minutes of tape, this student had word retrieval difficulties at least five times. Now she could further assess her student in this area.

Having the mentor help her to focus on specific aspects of her communication skills made it easier for Caitlin to analyze her tape thoroughly. She went on to write a brief reflection about how she met the CEC standard and provided written excerpts from her tape to support her justification.

Questions for Collaborative Reflection

For the mentor:

- Have I videotaped my own teaching recently? What do I stand to learn from watching a tape of my own classroom instruction?
- In analyzing the video- or audiotape of my mentee's teaching, did I remain objective and nonevaluative in my comments?
- What specific areas of my mentee's teaching, or my own, might better be reviewed through audiotaping rather than videotaping?
- In what other areas might the Sights and Sounds of the Classroom work as an observation strategy (add to Table 7-1)?

For the mentee:

- What did I learn about my teaching from audio- or videotaping?
- What did I learn about my students from audio- or videotaping?
- If I videotape my teaching at least three times during the year (once at the beginning, once in the middle, and once at the end), in which specific areas do I hope to see growth?
- In what other areas might the Sights and Sounds of the Classroom work as an observation strategy (add to Table 7-1)?

References

Evertson, C., Emmer, E., & Worsham, M. E. (2000). *Classroom management for elementary teachers* (5th ed.). Boston: Allyn and Bacon.

Ruddell, M. R. (2001). *Teaching content reading and writing* (3rd ed.). New York: Wiley.

8

The Link to Standards

In 1989 the National Governor's Association requested the development of national standards for learning and teaching, and in 1994 President Clinton signed the Goals 2000: Educate America Act. Since then, the term *standards* has been a constant focus of attention in the education arena. Professional organizations have created standards for their areas of expertise, individual states and districts have written or adopted standards, and accrediting associations are relying on a standards-based approval process of teacher education programs. With the push for accountability, standards are often used in determining teacher certification, licensing, and promotion (National Commission on Teaching and America's Future, 1997).

Beginning teacher standards can provide preservice and novice teachers with guidelines for acquiring effective teaching skills and knowledge. Standards can help to clarify what it takes to be successful in the classroom and can help new teachers to express clear expectations and long-term goals.

The Mentor's Link

How is your role as a mentor linked to the standards? As the mentor, you can support the new teacher in meeting standards for teaching excellence. You can provide demonstrations and examples from your own teaching that model standards-based practices. You can also brainstorm evidences that the two of you can collect to show that the new teacher has met some or all of the established standards. Many administrators are changing the way they evaluate a new teacher's performance. It used to be that a brief classroom observation would be enough, but more and more supervisors are using standards-based evaluation tools. It is in the best interest of your mentee to help him or her review the beginning teacher standards adopted by your state or district and any content or professional organization standards that also apply. The challenge to the mentor is to provide ample opportunity for the new teacher to practice implementing the standards, support the new teacher as he or she learns to meet the standards, and challenge him or her to go beyond the set expectations.

How do you as a mentor assist the new teacher in documenting that he or she has met the standards? Figure 8-1 outlines a possible procedure that you might use to follow a new teacher's journey to meet the standards. Using this process to show the strengths of a novice teacher could really give him or her the boost of confidence and reassurance that is often needed in the initial years and beyond. Begin by targeting one standard that is meaningful to the new teacher's situation. Then, together, list possible evidences or student products that could be gathered to show the teacher's accomplishment with the standard. Also, list any of the observation techniques discussed in this book or elsewhere that you could use to collect further data. Next, begin collecting and reviewing the multiple sources of evidence. Finally, decide as a team if the standard has been met or is still emerging. If the standard has been met, assist the mentee in documenting the evidence in his or her portfolio. If the new teacher is still in the emerging stage for a particular standard, set goals and action steps to help him or her progress ahead. Collaborative reflection should be ongoing throughout the entire process.

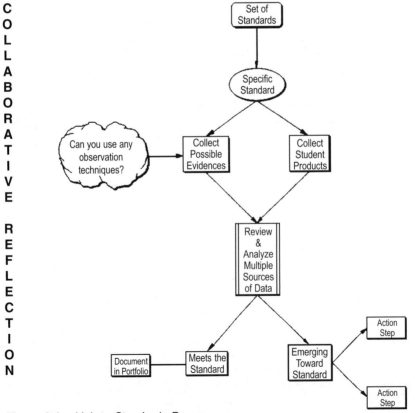

Figure 8-1. Link to Standards Process

It's not necessary to use this process for every standard that the new teacher is trying to reach, nor is it practical, given the hectic schedules under which teachers work. However, you can use the process in several ways: (a) Help the new teacher to reach a few standards that are linked to his or her professional goals for the year. (b) Select a few standards that the mentee wants to show growth in over the course of some time period. (c) Focus on the standards that the new teacher is successful with in order to support him or her during evaluation time.

Many national organizations, such as the National Board for Professional Teaching Standards and the Interstate New Teacher Assessment and Support Consortium (INTASC), have established standards for educators. In order to make our standards-link process more comprehensible, we have included an example in Appendix E using some of the INTASC standards (*INTASC Core Standards*, 2000). INTASC published 10 model standards for beginning educators in all disciplines and grade levels that have been adopted by many state departments of education and teacher education programs (Campbell, Melenyzer, Nettles, & Wyman, 2000). Although we have chosen to use these standards for our example, it is recommended that you use the teaching standards adopted by your particular district or state. In some cases, you may want to focus on content area standards established by professional organizations such as the National Council of Teachers of English (NCTE) or the National Council of Teachers of Mathematics (NCTM). For a list of professional organization Web sites with standards links, see Appendix F.

The Portfolio Link

Most candidates in a teacher education program compile some sort of portfolio to document their growth in the knowledge and skills required for teaching. Some teacher education programs use the portfolios for determining initial licensure, in preparation for job interviews, or both. In some cases these portfolios are used to document that certain beginning teacher standards and/or content standards have been met. Cooperating teachers, as mentors, play a vital role in helping student teachers to collect evidence of performance to the standards that can be incorporated into the portfolio. The challenge of maintaining the teaching portfolio and its practices continues in the first year that these new teachers accept a classroom of their own.

As the mentor, you can help the new teacher to maintain his or her professional portfolio and document his or her "history of learning to teach" (Lyons, 1999, p. 64). The evidence collected through your observations of the new teacher might be considered by the mentee as valuable to the portfolio. Other evidence or student work products gathered to support standards achievement might also be included. Most important, the ongoing reflection and the insights gained from your critical conversations are invaluable in making the portfolio more than just a scrapbook of accomplishments. The mentee should determine the purpose for maintaining the portfolio, and the mentor can be valuable in leading the mentee to choosing evidence that is meaningfully connected to standards of effective teaching. Shulman (1998) wrote, " A teaching portfolio is the structured, documentary history of a set of coached or mentored acts of teaching substantiated by samples of student work and fully realized only through reflective writing, deliberation, and serious conversation" (p. 37).

Final Thoughts

The accountability to standards can be intimidating for a new teacher who is still learning to manage the complex demands of facilitating a classroom. It can be a relief for the mentor to show the new teacher that what he or she is doing in instructional practice is already meeting one or more standards. It can also be calming for the new teacher to know that a mentor, in the journey to develop the skills and knowledge essential to being a master teacher, supports him or her. Linking practice to standards can be professional development for both mentor and mentee.

Questions for Collaborative Reflection

For the mentor:

- What is my personal philosophy about beginning teacher standards?
- How have I implemented the standards associated with the professional organizations of which I am a member?
- How might I incorporate the expectations from the National Board for Professional Teaching Standards into my own classroom practices?
- Do I have my own updated teaching portfolio? If not, how can I begin to compile my own teaching portfolio? How can I use my relationship with my mentee to strengthen the learning process of constructing both of our portfolios? If I do have a portfolio, is it meaningfully connected to teaching standards?

For the mentee:

- Which specific standards do I want to target during this particular school year?
- How are these standards linked to my professional goals?
- What professional development opportunities are available to help me obtain these standards?
- How can I incorporate my mentor's suggestions into my teaching portfolio and classroom practices?

References

Campbell, D., Melenyzer, B., Nettles, D., & Wyman, R. (2000). *Portfolio and performance assessment in teacher education.* Needham Heights, MA: Allyn & Bacon.

INTASC core standards. (2000, August 10). Washington, DC: Council of Chief State School Officers. Available on-line: http://www.ccsso.org/intascst.html

Lyons, N. (1999). How portfolios can shape emerging practice. *Educational Leadership, 56* (8), 63–65.

National Commission on Teaching and America's Future. (1997). *Doing what matters most: Investing in quality teaching.* New York: Columbia University Teachers College.

Shulman, L. (1998). Teacher portfolios. In N. Lyons (Ed.), *With portfolio in hand: Validating the new teacher professionalism.* New York: Teachers College Press.

9

The Link to
Professional Development

Stephen Covey (1989) revealed the seven habits of highly effective people. Habit number 7 is called "Sharpen the Saw: Principles of Balanced Self-Renewal." Effective people take time to renew themselves physically, mentally, emotionally, socially, and spiritually. For educators it is vital that they renew their enthusiasm for teaching, expand upon existing knowledge and skills, and reflect upon daily practices.

Have you ever attended a conference or read an educational book that was so interesting that you were immediately motivated to go out and implement those ideas or research them for yourself? Maybe you've attended workshops where the information presented was not so new to you, but it reaffirmed the importance of the practices you hold dear in your classroom. In either case, you probably felt rejuvenated and motivated after having the opportunity to converse and share ideas with colleagues. It's no surprise that at international educational conventions, thousands of educators turn out to present their own ideas and learn from each other. Professional development is one way that educators "sharpen the saw" and maintain the energy and creativity required to teach.

The fact that you are, or considering becoming, a mentor confirms your desire for professional development. In fact, if you were selected to be a mentor in your district, one of the reasons may very well be the fact that you continue to be a lifelong learner. Routman (1996) writes, " I believe mentoring and supporting other teachers is a professional responsibility. The only way we continue to grow is to support, teach, and share with each other" (p. 175). The ability to guide a new professional toward achieving his or her professional goals is both a challenge and a gift.

The Need for Professional Development

The federal government recognized the need for continuing professional development when it enacted the Goals 2000: Educate America Act in 1994. One of the goals of this legislation deals specifically with designing and implementing quality professional development for teachers. The National Commission on Teaching and America's Future (1996) also emphasized the same need in its report entitled "What Matters Most: Teaching for America's Future." The report makes five connected recommendations for improving the quality of teaching and learning. Part of recommendation number 2 is reinventing professional development. The Commission recommended that mentoring programs be established for new teachers "that provide support and assess teaching skills." It also emphasized the need for all teachers to "have access to high quality learning opportunities."

The challenges in today's classrooms can seem insurmountable if teachers aren't able to converse with colleagues and engage in problem solving. The increasing class sizes and different ability levels place sometimes overwhelming demands on teachers. The growing diversity in our classrooms makes it necessary for teachers to become familiar with the customs, traditions, and languages that are part of their students' lives. The demand for students to be adequately prepared to use technology requires teachers to keep up with the rapid advances in that area. In addition, the inclusion of children with special needs into the general education classroom is one more reason for teachers to keep updating their skills and refining their methods. Special education teachers have the added challenge of keeping abreast of the continually outdated paperwork requirements for IEPs, assessments, and team meetings. The field of education is changing so rapidly, and new philosophies, methods, and ideas are springing up constantly. Educators not only have to be teachers, they have to be learners as well.

Collaborative Professional Development

A mentoring relationship is the perfect venue for collaborative professional development. "Teachers are more likely to take risks when they trust and feel supported by their fellow educators" (Routman, 1996, p. 174). Together, a mentor and mentee can identify target areas that are applicable to their own classrooms and support one another as they undergo the change process. Personally selecting issues that are relevant to your classroom ensures that you will be committed to seeking answers and that the process will be meaningful. The collaborative relationship allows for the two teachers to help each other find resources, dialogue about what is working and what is not, and problem-solve together. Research also states that for professional development to bring about lasting, positive change it has to be "suffused throughout the teachers' working lives" (Renyi, 1998, p. 71). Engaging in professional development together ensures that theory is continually being discussed, modeled, and practiced. By conducting observations in each other's classrooms, the mentor and mentee can formally debrief teaching practices and understandings with one another (Ayers & Schubert, 1994). They can also support one another's reflective practices. "In teaching, as in life, maximizing meaning from experiences requires reflection" (Costa & Kallick, 2000, p. 61). In the next section, we discuss some methods that you and your mentee might want to try together.

Suggestions for
Collaborative Professional Development

Figure 9-1 illustrates some methods of collaborative professional development. These are only a few suggestions; there are many more you could add to this list. What matters is that you and your mentee find the form of professional development that you are both comfortable undertaking.

Figure 9-1. Collaborative Professional Development

Shared Reading

One way that educators keep abreast of new topics in the field is reading professional journals. Maybe there's a particular journal that interests both you and your mentee and is related to your particular subject area or area of expertise. Read selected articles and discuss them at one of your conference times together. You might also seek out specific books or research articles that will be helpful with the area you or your mentee targeted for professional development. Remember to keep a list of the journals and books you read for your portfolio. In addition, you might want to write a brief blurb about what it is you gained from the reading and how it influenced what you do in your classroom.

Attending Conferences

Have you attended any local, national, or international conventions? Do you remember the first time that you did? Maybe another teacher invited you, or vice versa. Sometimes new teachers are intimidated by the thought of attending a conference on their own, even if it truly piques their interest. As a mentor, you can invite your mentee to go along with you to a professional convention or offer to go along with him or her. The two of you can critique the information you've learned at different sessions, network with other educators, and bring the information back to share with others in the school or district. If you are a member of an organization that sponsors such conventions, such as the National Council of Teachers of English or the Council for Exceptional Children, share that information with your mentee and help him or her to obtain membership in an organization of choice.

Writing Proposals/Presenting

When I (Marlene) first began teaching at Salve Regina, a fellow colleague and informal mentor of mine invited me to go along with her to the Council for Exceptional Children Convention being held in North Carolina. My colleague, Alice, was a presenter and as I sat in on her session I thought that I'd like to present here next year. Alice is the one who guided me through writing my first proposal. She handed me one of hers as a sample and discussed with me my ideas for topics to present. She later read my finished proposal, gave me some feedback, and off it went. I was elated when I found out that the proposal had been accepted. Whenever I remember that experience, I think of Alice as my mentor.

Teachers must be leaders in the field of education. You can empower your mentee to become a teacher leader by jointly writing and submitting a proposal. If you can't go to a national or an international convention, identify a local one. Present together on a topic you've been discussing and trying in your classrooms. If you've been asked to present at a workshop, involve your mentee in the preparation so that he or she can get a handle on the practical aspects such as creating handouts, structuring the time, varying the methods, and arranging the setting.

Committee Service

Part of the job of an educator is to serve on various committees that make decisions about teaching and learning. There's always an opportunity to serve in parent-teacher organizations, on curriculum committees, or on pilot material committees. A mentee can benefit by serving on the same committee as the mentor and observing him or her in action. If that's not possible, then as a mentor you can share a little information about the role of each committee and its task so that the new teacher can choose one that is best suited to him or her.

Classroom Visitations

Sometimes, when educators are trying a new technique in their classrooms, they question whether they are implementing it correctly because they've never really seen it in action. If possible, with administrative support, arrange for you and your mentee to visit other classrooms where the new technique you are implementing is already in use effectively. Seeing another teacher use the technique under conditions similar to your own makes it realistically achievable.

Grant Writing

Grant writing is something that a novice teacher most likely won't have much experience with unless he or she has had the opportunity to work with grants in a previous career. There are many veteran teachers who have never written a grant. Grants are available to educators and are usually advertised in educational journals, on educational organization Web sites, and in books devoted just to grants for teachers. Although many grants have specific requirements, there might be a grant that would suit some idea you or your mentee have wanted to try. Even better, you might find a grant that would support some collaborative project for both of you. In any case, the process of seeking out grants and learning to write one efficiently is a form of professional development that you can pursue together.

Teacher Research

"Teacher research means seeing what has been in front of us all the time. It means seeing something we didn't expect to see, a sure sign of learning since what we expect is what we already know" (Bissex, 1994, p. 90). Teacher research may not be something to do at the beginning of the mentee's first year, but it is certainly an advanced form of professional development for the two of you to undertake toward the end of the first year or in his or her second year of teaching. Teacher research usually stems from wanting to solve a problem, answer a question, or discover the effects of a new methodology. If the new teacher has put some of his or her identified action plans into effect in the classroom, the two of you may want to engage in teacher research to evaluate the results. Bissex recommends that all that's needed to begin teacher research is an inquisitive mind and some simple tools, such as a notebook, audio- or videotapes of the classroom, and student interviews. " For experienced teachers, teacher research provides an avenue for professional renewal and growth; for all teachers, including those just beginning, it offers a way of learning with dignity from our experiences" (p. 103).

Reflection

Throughout this book we have emphasized the need to be reflective. We know that reflection is often overlooked because it takes time, a factor that is all too scarce in the life of an educator. Sincere reflection is not easy because it goes deeper than looking at the surface events that take place in our classrooms. It also requires examining our own beliefs, attitudes, and actions. Reflection can take the form of writing in a personal or dialogue journal, or simply having a conversation. "To be reflective means to mentally wander through where you have been and to try [to] make sense of it" (Costa & Kallick, 2000, p. 61). Being a mentor requires you to reflect on your own beliefs, actions, and philosophy. It also requires that you listen as your mentee reflects on the same.

Final Thoughts

New teachers often enter the field with a sense of excitement and a desire to soak up all the new ideas and skills they can as they teach. Engaging in some form of professional development ensures that the teaching is always fresh and never predictable. Teaching remains exciting as long as teachers continue to learn and implement new techniques.

Questions for Collaborative Reflection

For mentor and mentee:

- What are some areas of teaching that you would like to develop further through professional development?
- Where might you find resources or professional development opportunities to support your interests?
- How can you support one another through the process of implementing change based on your professional development experiences?

References

Ayers, W., & Schubert, W. (1994). Teacher lore: Learning about teaching from teachers. In T. Shanahan (Ed.), *Teachers thinking, teachers knowing* (pp. 105–121). Urbana, IL: National Council of Teachers of English.

Bissex, G. (1994). Teacher research: Seeing what we are doing. In T. Shanahan (Ed.), *Teachers thinking, teachers knowing* (pp. 88–104). Urbana, IL: National Council of Teachers of English.

Costa, A., & Kallick, B. (2000). Getting into the habit of reflection. *Educational Leadership, 57* (7), 60–62.

Covey, S. R. (1989). *The 7 habits of highly effective people: Powerful lessons in personal change.* New York: Simon & Schuster.

National Commission on Teaching and America's Future. (1996). *What matters most: Teaching for America's future.* New York: Author.

Renyi, J. (1998). Building learning into the teaching job. *Educational Leadership, 55* (5), 70–74.

Routman, R. (1996). *Literacy at the crossroads: Crucial talk about reading, writing, and other teaching dilemmas.* Portsmouth, NH: Heinemann.

10

A Mentor and
Mentee in Action

We've covered many of the important aspects of mentoring in this book. We've discussed reflection, conferences, observations, analysis, standards, and professional development. Through the vignettes in each chapter we've tried to represent what these aspects might look like in an actual mentoring relationship. Most of what we've discussed is readily applicable to mentoring the novice teacher, but what if your mentee is not a novice at all? Some districts are assigning mentors to teachers who are new to the district or school building but not new to teaching. What then? In this chapter we briefly explore another angle of mentoring by interviewing a mentor and a mentee who are in that situation. Their insights into the mentoring relationship confirm what we have suggested throughout the book and offer new advice for mentors who are working with experienced teachers.

Mentor and Mentee Backgrounds

It was 7 a.m. and the halls of the large middle school were deserted, but Leonore Rizy and her mentee, Erica Bulk, were eager to meet with us and share their mentoring story. Leonore has been teaching full time for 21 years. She has been in her current position as a special educator in the sixth grade since 1985. Just recently, Leonore earned the title and respect of National Board Certified Teacher. Erica is in her third year of teaching. After earning her undergraduate degree in elementary and special education, she worked with middle school students who were behaviorally challenged in a hospital-based classroom setting. The next year, she moved her classroom to the middle school she is currently in, still teaching students with challenging behaviors but not employed by the local district. Currently, she has transitioned into an eighth-grade special education position and is employed by the same district and school as Leonore. Leonore became Erica's official mentor.

The Mentoring Relationship

Leonore has been an official mentor for her district's program for the past 3 years. However, she noted that before the district's mentoring program was officially in place, she was already assisting new teachers in the building. In the past 3 years she has not had a mentee who was a brand-new teacher; she has worked with many mentees who have some experience but are new to the school or district. In fact, one year she mentored a teacher who had several years experience but was changing grade levels and curriculum. In Leonore's school district, "teachers are supported for any change." Some of the aspects of mentoring an experienced teacher are the same as with a new teacher, such as acquainting him or her with the physical plant and the staff and faculty members. However, Leonore finds that with an experienced teacher changing environments, emotional support is most critical.

Leonore admits that her recently earned title, as National Board Certified Teacher, seems to have brought with it professional respect. "We all learn, and I want to continue to learn, too, but you can see that the level of rapport has changed; it's better." She says it's like "wearing a stamp on your head," and your ideas and professional opinions are not challenged as often. Although she doesn't believe that it has affected her role as a mentor, we disagree. Given the countless hours she had to spend analyzing her own teaching, reflecting on her classroom practices, and collecting documentation of her teaching and professional development, it seems that she would be very understanding and helpful for other teachers who do the same.

Leonore has been trained by the district to be a mentor. She says that the structure of the mentoring program "depends on the needs of the mentee." In her training Leonore has been advised to support a teacher through issues that "emotionally might send them out the door." The training also stressed confidentiality. Leonore believes that it is vital for the mentee to know that together they will work out issues on a personal level, without involving administration or evaluating anything. Mentor-mentee discussions are sometimes a venue for safe "venting."

Erica is quite proficient at what she does and needs more support in the area of legal issues in special education and paperwork, such as writing IEPs. Leonore stated, "Some teachers have been ready to bail, and they need help ironing out personal issues or chain of command issues." Erica's issues have revolved more around changing special education laws, program issues, and child issues. Leonore is the perfect mentor for this situation because she has been teaching special education since before the law was enacted. She is able to share her personal history of what teaching was like before and after special education law with young teachers like Erica. Although Erica admits that Leonore is very knowledgeable in answering her questions, Leonore says she doesn't always know the answers, but she knows where they can both go to find them.

Characteristics of an Effective Mentor

Leonore stated three characteristics of an effective mentor. The first and most important to her is that a mentor can put the mentee at ease. The mentor needs to set up a "no-risk situation" in which the mentee knows that anything said is confidential. Establishing a comfort level of safety is a priority. If the mentee thinks that you will violate confidentiality, then he or she may not feel safe coming to you for support. Second, a mentor has to be knowledgeable in his or her discipline, in teaching, and in being a mentor. Third, objectivity is a must! The mentor has to be able to keep an open mind and problem solve objectively.

Erica believes it is critical that a mentor be available when the mentee needs help. Erica mimics her mentor: "We need to meet. We need to meet." She admits that sometimes she has nothing to discuss with her mentor. Yet when she gets to the meeting, things come up and they usually spend almost an hour conversing. She also listed one of the characteristics of an effective mentor as someone who is "welcoming." In addition, she thinks it is imperative that if a mentoring relationship is going to work, the two teachers should be in the same discipline. "Some of the new teachers feel disconnected. Leonore and I are both in special education, and we can connect in that way." Having a mentor who is in one discipline and a mentee who is in another makes mentoring difficult. Leonore has experienced that scenario in the past and says the challenge is that you don't know each other's curriculum, so it's hard to support someone in that area.

Both Leonore and Erica feel the frustration of trying to find a common time to meet. They are on different schedules for planning and lunch, which makes it hard to get together during the day. Erica teaches after-school programs, and both of them have families to attend to after school. They don't sacrifice their meeting times, though. Leonore creatively rearranges her schedule so that she can meet with Erica during her planning time, or they come in early, as they did for this interview.

The Role of Observation and Reflection

In their district, the teachers are allowed to take visitation days. Teachers can use those days to visit another classroom, school, or district. If a mentor or mentee feels the need to observe or be observed, a visitation day is used. Novice teachers seem to need more observation than experienced teachers who are being mentored. Erica notes that she's comfortable with her teaching now, but during her first year she would have welcomed the opportunity to observe a master teacher. Unfortunately, Erica did not have a mentor her first year, and she says that if she had Leonore back then, she would have definitely shadowed her.

Thinking back to the demanding task of earning National Board certification, Leonore emphasizes the importance of reflection. In her own practice, "reflection is ongoing"; it is a normal part of her day. In the mentoring relationship, the two reflect on their discussions and their problem-solving techniques. Erica says that after she has met with Leonore and they've agreed on an action plan for a particular issue, she puts it into place. Then, at the next meeting, Leonore will ask, " How did that work?" This opens up a dialogue for revisiting their plan and making changes if necessary or celebrating success. Leonore often reflects on how she handles situations that come up with Erica. She uses a lot of self-questioning: "How can I be more helpful to her? Did I do the right thing? Is what I said clear and accurate? Should I get more information to her? What resources can I give her?"

The Role of Standards

During Erica's evaluation this year by her building administrator, she had a preconference with him, an observation, and then a postconference. Although she did not have to specify certain standards she was meeting, she knows that that will soon change. Leonore knows that change in the evaluation process is forthcoming: "They [administrators] are beginning to evaluate you on a set of specific teaching standards." In fact, in some nearby districts, administrators are already doing just that. When Erica began her new position, she attended a 3-day workshop on standards based teaching. Both Leonore and Erica recognize that supporting each other in the standards process will have to become another component of the mentoring relationship.

The Role of Professional Development

Leonore and Erica could have spoken all day about their professional development experiences. Both of them are highly motivated teachers who are continually striving to learn new skills and methods that will make their teaching effective. Leonore has obviously spent numerous hours in professional development simply through the process of National Board certification. She doesn't stop there though; she's already scheduled to attend an all-day workshop on Patricia Cunningham's Four Block Literacy Program. She has a purpose in mind for attending this conference: she hopes to be working with a team of teachers in her building who use this program, and she has a strong desire to implement it meaningfully. Attending the conference will ensure that she gets an overview of the whole program rather than fragments. Erica is already scheduled to attend a 3-day workshop over the summer. One of the things she hopes to gain from that conference is leadership skills. The district they work in really encourages professional development. Erica and Leonore have jointly attended district-sponsored conferences and workshops. "They [the district administrators] want you constantly learning." These two teachers will support each other when they come back from the workshops and begin to implement changes in their classrooms.

Successes and Challenges

Leonore and Erica have encountered successes in their mentoring experience. Both teachers feel strongly that trust is what makes their relationship work. There is no hierarchy to the relationship. Sometimes it is Leonore who needs to get advice from the younger teachers like Erica. In addition, the fact that they are both in the same discipline (special education) bonds them together and allows them to "bounce" ideas off one another.

However, Leonore and Erica have faced some challenges as well—for example, time. There's just not enough to go around! Leonore and Erica are frustrated when they can't find a time to meet or collaborate. Leonore stated, "If we had the time, we could even do more." They both value their meetings and consider them a necessary component of the program. "You may not always meet with a specific agenda, but things do come up when you sit together." So, although time is a challenge, they don't give up. Their support network for each other is too valuable to discard.

Final Thoughts

Leonore offered some advice for a mentee: "Never be afraid to ask. Never be afraid to research the answer. You are a continual learner. Seeking out answers in collaboration with others makes a good teacher." In the same light, Erica suggested a piece of advice for mentors: "Keep your door open. Be approachable and welcoming."

Finally, Leonore concluded our interview with a powerful statement: "As a mentor you are helping your profession by keeping quality people in it!"

11

 Putting It All Together

This book opened with the display of a want ad looking for qualified mentors. We sincerely hope that after reading this book and reflecting on the benefits of the position, you will accept the job. It was our intention in this book to equip you with some "tools of the trade" to use in your mentoring relationship. Some of those tools include conferencing ideas, observation techniques, a connection to standards-based teaching, and professional development suggestions. In addition, we also sought to stimulate the habit of reflection for both you and your mentee. We hope that the questions for collaborative reflection and analysis at the end of the chapters will help you both to reflect on your own practice and educational philosophy.

In thinking about the mentoring relationship, we can use the analogy of hiking up a steep mountainside. The mentee is the novice hiker and you (the mentor) are the experienced trail guide. Prior to arriving at this point, the hiker has prepared by fitting him- or herself with the appropriate gear, learning how to use the hiking aids available, watching videos or reading books on the subject, and hiking through easier mountain trails. In the same way, the novice teacher has prepared through participation in teacher education courses, collecting resources, and student teaching. Both are somewhat unfamiliar with the territory they are about to enter, whether it is a mountain or a school environment.

As the trail guide, you lead your mentee through the hiking trails as you begin the ascent up the steep mountain. Along the way you suggest the best paths to follow and clarifying your reasoning. You explain a little of the history of the mountain (school) and its surroundings. You watch the novice climber's techniques and offer helpful tips to make the journey easier, or model your own skills. As you both make your way to the peak of the mountain, there may be some trials, like bad weather, covered trails, and injuries, that cause interference. As the experienced guide, you try to minimize these interferences so that the new climber can focus on reaching his or her goal. You problem-solve along the way, involving the novice in all decisions. With each step, the novice hiker feels more comfortable and safe under your direction.

Finally, you both reach the peak. The air is refreshing and the view is breathtaking. Both of you stop and pause as you reflect back on the hike to the summit. With a newfound confidence and sharpened skills, the novice now takes the lead for the descent. The hike down is much easier because of all that was learned and gained from the hike up. By the time the two of you reach the bottom, you are walking side by side, conversing and planning for your next adventure together. It is evident to you already that in a few years this novice hiker will become a guide for someone else embarking on the journey for the first time. For the novice, he or she will always have the memory of the first climb to the summit of a mountain and the one who led him or her there.

Advice for Mentors

There are so many facets to the mentoring relationship that it is impossible to offer you a script to follow in your new role. Each school environment is different, every mentor and mentee has a unique personality, and people have various experiences and hold different philosophies. That's why it is so important that, to nourish the relationship with your mentee, you find what works best in your situation. In our interview (see chapter 10), Leonore and Erica offered some excellent advice for mentors. Erica emphasized the importance of a mentor being "available and welcoming." Leonore stressed the need for the mentoring relationship to be confidential and objective. Both teachers agreed that establishing a comfort level between the two professionals is a priority.

A report produced by the National Academy of Sciences, the National Academy of Engineering, and the Institute of Medicine (1997) offered ideas for new mentors. The following is a sample from their list of advice:

- Listen patiently
- Build a relationship
- Nurture self-sufficiency
- Establish protected time
- Share yourself
- Be constructive
- Find your own mentors

Although the report is aimed at mentoring students in science and engineering, the advice is applicable to all mentors, no matter what the teaching field may be. Their advice can be related to the focus of this book.

Listen patiently.   One of the most meaningful qualities a mentor should hold is that of being an active listener. A mentee needs to be able to express him- or herself on matters that are professional, social, and emotional and be assured that the mentor is listening nonjudgmentally. It is also vital that the mentor listen without disrupting and allow the mentee to completely share his or her thoughts. Being a patient listener shows that you value the mentee's concerns and contributions.

Build a relationship. This advice will be easier to implement for mentors and mentees who have built-in time to spend together. However, in chapter 9 we offered several professional development opportunities that will encourage relationship building. Finding any shared personal interests or hobbies will also strengthen the professional relationship you build together.

Nurture self-sufficiency. Just as in the analogy of the hiker, as mentors we eventually want our mentees to become the guides for future new educators. In order to accomplish that goal, mentors should nurture self-sufficiency. Collecting evidence that demonstrates the new teacher's competencies toward meeting specific standards instills the new teacher with a sense of pride and accomplishment that is necessary for making independent decisions and taking risks (see chapter 8).

Establish protected time. "Protected time" can be difficult to find in some instances. Time must be set aside for the mentor and mentee to confer and dialogue together without numerous disruptions. Amid all the responsibilities given to teachers, it is often hard to make the time to sit together and talk. New teachers have so many things to learn and issues to deal with that they often think they don't have time to meet with their mentor. Yet the whole notion of mentoring is that talking to one another and brainstorming might alleviate many of these same issues and concerns. It becomes the mentor's task to encourage that time together and be certain that it is "protected."

Share yourself. "Let your...[mentee] know about your successes and failures and encourage them to reciprocate" (National Academy of Sciences et. al., 1997). We all started out as novices, and we all had our share of trials and tribulations. Let your mentee know that you remember what it was like to begin your teaching career and how you dealt with similar issues. Also, share your history. If you are a veteran teacher who has experienced dynamic changes in the history of education, share those interesting stories with your mentee. While interviewing Leonore and Erica, I was spellbound as Leonore recounted her days of teaching before special education laws existed. Her memories were interesting and informative and allowed her mentee to appreciate how far the quality of education for students with special needs has progressed.

Be constructive. Throughout this book we have tried to accent the constructive nature of observing one another's teaching, collecting data, and analyzing that data collaboratively. A mentor is not an evaluator.

Nor should a mentor want a new teacher to simply replicate the mentor's teaching style. The aim is to nurture the novice by identifying his or her own strengths and building upon those. The observation techniques discussed in this book are intended to be used to identify needs and document successes.

Find your own mentors.   If mentoring is a new venture for you, it might be beneficial for you to seek out colleagues in your own district who have experienced mentoring, officially or unofficially. These teachers will provide you with what works and what doesn't, given the uniqueness of your own school or district environment. These are the people who can probably offer you the most valuable advice of all.

Additional resources on mentoring are continually emerging. Many professional organizations, such as the Council for Exceptional Children, are in the process of drafting quality standards for mentoring practice. Begin by contacting the professional organizations you are associated with or visiting their Web sites for current information on mentoring programs. Then research the initiatives taken by your state department of education on the issue of mentoring. Finally, if you haven't already done so, determine if training opportunities exist for mentors in your own school district.

Conclusion

We genuinely hope that this book has reaffirmed your choice to become a mentor. We hope we have been able to offer you something new to think about or implement in your mentoring position. Do not underestimate the value of the role you have accepted and its influence on the professionalism of teaching and the quality of instruction in our schools.

Final Thoughts

A mentor is:

- Someone who shares thoughts, ideas, material, and expertise
- A collaborator who keeps an open mind and a nonjudgmental view
- One who listens patiently and confers privately
- An objective observer who maintains confidentiality
- A reflective practitioner who analyzes his or her own teaching
- A friend

The mentoring relationship fosters:

- Professional development individually and cooperatively
- Self-renewal of both teachers, which revitalizes the joy of teaching
- Constructive feedback and the habit of reflection
- The change process, through support, guidance, and reflection

Mentoring enhances:

- The retention of outstanding teachers for our students
- Professional goal setting for the immediate and distant future
- Classroom instruction through careful analysis of teaching
- Standards-based practices
- The overall school's climate by modeling the power of collaborative spirit

Reference

National Academy of Sciences, National Academy of Engineering, & the Institute of Medicine. (1997) *Adviser, teacher, role model, friend: On being a mentor to students in science and engineering.* Washington, DC: National Academy Press.

Word for Word Form

Mentee's Name:

Mentor's Name:

Date of Observation:

Subject of Lesson:

Target Area for Observation:

* While observing the area of concern targeted by the new teacher, write down exactly what is said by the teacher, word for word, within this area.

Notes from Discussion:

Possible Action Steps:

B

Measuring Methodology Matrix—Mentor Observation

Directions: On the matrix, fill in the date along the top row, and list the methods used by the mentee along the left column. In the boxes, the mentee can use the key provided to rate the method and include any comments. Additional comments, from mentor or mentee, can be listed at the bottom of the form.

Methodology Focus:
Instructional—Grouping—Assessment—Classroom Management—Other _____

DAY/DATE

METHODS						

Key:
Mostly Effective = ✔+
Somewhat Effective = ✔
Ineffective = ✔−

Additional comments:

C

Measuring Methodology Matrix—Mentee Self-Assessment

Directions: On the matrix, fill in the date along the top row, and list the methods you plan to use or have used for the week along the left column. In the boxes, use the key provided to rate the method and include any comments. Additional comments can be listed at the bottom of the form. (For an example of a completed matrix, see Appendix D).

Methodology Focus:
Instructional—Grouping—Assessment—Classroom Management—Other _____

	DAY/DATE				
	MON /	TUES /	WED /	THURS /	FRI /
METHODS					

Key:
Mostly Effective = ✔+
Somewhat Effective = ✔
Ineffective = ✔−

Additional comments:

Measuring Methodology in Action Matrix

Methodology Focus:
Instructional—Grouping—Assessment—Classroom Management—Other Standards

		MON 10/22	TUES 10/23	WED 10/24	THURS 10/25	FRI 10/26
METHODS	Problem Solving		✔+	✔ Didn't allow enough time	✔+	
	Representations		✔+ Elicits thoughtful questions			✔+
	District Math Text	✔+				✔+ A good overview
	Computer Software					
	Calculators/ Manipulatives/Aids	✔+	✔+ Next, try to predict first and then check	✔+	✔+ Calculators in pairs— success!	
	Engagement in Math Discourse		✔+ Effective intro. to lesson	✔+ Stimulated interest		
	Modeling	✔+ "Think aloud" was engaging	✔+			
	Independent Practice				✔+	✔+ Effective supplement to text review
	Application			✔+ Would this work with groups too?	✔+	
	Student Reflection	✔ Enough time? Limited depth				✔ Still not comfortable

DAY/DATE

Key:
Mostly Effective = ✔+
Somewhat Effective = ✔
Ineffective = ✔–

Additional comments: I was unable to integrate technology again this week. I still feel uncomfortable with the student reflection, and I think this is affecting the students' performance in this area.

Appendix

E

INTASC
Standards/Sample Evidences

INTASC Core Standard

Principle #1: The teacher understands the central concepts, tools of inquiry, and structures of the discipline(s) he or she teaches and can create learning experiences that make these aspects of subject matter meaningful for students.

Performance: The teacher effectively uses multiple representations and explanations of disciplinary concepts that capture key ideas and link them to students' prior understandings.

Evidence

- Lesson Plans
- Observation Technique #1 – Word for Word
- Observation Technique #4 – Measuring Methodology
- Observation Technique #5 – Sights and Sounds
- _____
- _____
- _____

INTASC Core Standard

Principle #3: The teacher understands how students differ in their approaches to learning and creates instructional opportunities that are adapted to diverse learners.

Performance: The teacher makes appropriate provisions (in terms of time and circumstances for work, tasks assigned, communication and response modes) for individual students who have particular learning differences or needs.

Evidence

- Lesson Plans with Noted Modifications
- Observation Technique #2 – Keeping Track of Time
- Observation Technique #4 – Measuring Methodology
- Observation Technique #5 – Sights and Sounds
- _____
- _____
- _____

INTASC Core Standard	**Evidence**
Principle #5: The teacher uses an understanding of individual and group motivation and behavior to create a learning environment that encourages positive social interaction, active engagement in learning, and self-motivation. Performance: The teacher organizes, allocates, and manages the resources of time, space, activities, and attention to provide active and equitable engagement of students in productive tasks.	• Observation Technique #1 – Word for Word • Observation Technique #2 – Keeping Track of Time • Observation Technique #3 – Mapping the Classroom • Observation Technique #5 – Sights and Sounds • _____ • _____ • _____

INTASC Core Standard	**Evidence**
Principle #6: The teacher uses knowledge of effective verbal, nonverbal, and media communication techniques to foster active inquiry, collaboration, and supportive interaction in the classroom. Performance: The teacher knows how to use a variety of media communication tools, including audiovisual aids and computers, to enrich learning opportunities.	• Attendance at Workshops • Teacher-Made Web Pages • Observation Technique #4 – Measuring Methodology • Observation Technique #5 – Sights and Sounds • _____ • _____ • _____

INTASC Core Standard	**Evidence**
Principle #8: The teacher understands and uses formal and informal assessment strategies to evaluate and ensure the continuous intellectual, social, and physical development of the learner. Performance: The teacher appropriately uses a variety of formal and informal assessment techniques (e.g., observation, portfolios of student work, teacher-made tests, performance tasks, projects, student self-assessments, peer assessment, and standardized tests) to enhance her or his knowledge of learners, evaluate students' progress and performances, and modify teaching and learning strategies.	• Sample Assessments • Assessment Reports • Anecdotal Records • Copies of Student Portfolios • Observation Technique #4 – Measuring Methodology • _____ • _____ • _____

INTASC Core Standard

Principle #9: The teacher is a reflective practitioner who continually evaluates the effects of his or her choices and actions on others (students, parents, and other professionals in the learning community) and who actively seeks out opportunities to grow professionally.

Performance: The teacher draws upon professional colleagues within the school and other professional arenas as supports for reflection, problem-solving and new ideas, actively sharing experiences and seeking and giving feedback.

Evidence

- Participation in a Mentoring Program
- Reflective Journal
- Professional Portfolio
- Data from any of the Observation Techniques
- _____
- _____
- _____

The following is a list of professional organizations with standards links:

✔ American Association of School Librarians
   http://www.ala.org/aasl/ip_nine.html

✔ American Council on the Teaching of Foreign Languages
   http://www.actfl.org/

✔ Association for Career and Technical Education
   http://www.avaonline.org/

✔ Council for Exceptional Children
   http://www.cec.sped.org/index.html

✔ International Technology Education Association
   http://www.iteawww.org/

✔ The Interstate New Teacher Assessment and Support Consortium
   http://www.ccsso.org/intascst.html

✔ National Association for Bilingual Education
   http://www.nabe.org/

✔ National Association for Music Education
   http://www.menc.org/publication/books/prek12st.html

✔ National Association for Sport and Physical Education
   http://www.aahperd.org/naspe/publications-nationalstandards.html#list

✔ National Art Education Association
   http://www.naea-reston.org/

✔ National Board for Professional Teaching Standards
   http://www.nbpts.org/

✔ National Center for Health Education
  http://www.nche.org/

✔ National Council for Accreditation of Teacher Education
  http://www.ncate.org/standard/m_stds.htm

✔ National Council for the Social Studies
  http://www.socialstudies.org/standards/

✔ National Council of Teachers of English
  http://www.ncte.org/standards/

✔ National Council of Teachers of Mathematics
  http://www.nctm.org/standards/

✔ National Science Education Standards
  http://books.nap.edu/html/nses/html/index.html

✔ Teachers of English to Speakers of Other Languages
  http://www.tesol.org/assoc/k12standards/it/01.html

About the Authors

Marlene P. Correia is the Special Education Program Coordinator at Salve Regina University in Newport, Rhode Island. She is currently a doctoral candidate in the Language Arts and Literacy Program at University of Massachusetts Lowell. Marlene has worked as a classroom teacher, special educator, mentor teacher, and university instructor in preservice teacher education. She has presented at local, national, and international conferences and has earned the honor of Professionally Recognized Special Educator by the Council for Exceptional Children.

Jana M. McHenry is the Reading Specialist at the A. B. Cushman School in Dartmouth, Massachusetts. She is currently a doctoral candidate in the Language Arts and Literacy Program at University of Massachusetts Lowell. Jana has worked as a classroom teacher, cooperating teacher, community college instructor, and university adjunct faculty in both preservice teacher education and professional development for local educators. She has presented at several conferences and serves as a Review Team Member for *The Reading Teacher.*

Index